DATE DUE

APR 2 8 2005		

Demco, Inc. 38-293

The Intellectual
and the Market Place

The Intellectual
and the Market Place

AND OTHER ESSAYS

George J. Stigler

THE FREE PRESS OF GLENCOE

Collier-Macmillan Limited, London

PREFACE

A PREFACE is designed to entice and disarm the reader,—two not wholly harmonious goals. The ingenuity of man has contrived infinitely varied advertisements, as prefaces once were more candidly labelled. But they fall generally into two classes. The one class makes such bold claims that the reader feels compelled to read the book in order to denounce it. The other class, written with an arm wrenched by importunate friends, is so modest as to entice by suspicion.

This slender volume would more appropriately have the latter type of preface, if I could only find the importunate friends. It deals with academic questions, both general and economic. All of the essays are lightly written, usually with an attempt to amuse, and perhaps sometimes with success.

CONTENTS

PREFACE   *v*

FOREWORD, *George P. Shultz*   ix

Part One
MOSTLY ABOUT UNIVERSITIES

1   An Academic Episode   *1*

2   Specialism: A DISSENTING OPINION   9

3   The National Commission as an Instrument
     of Controlled Impartiality   *17*

4   Stigler's First Law of Sympathy   *25*

5   Festschriften   *31*

6   Meager Means and Noble Ends   33

Part Two
ALL ABOUT ECONOMICS

7   Stigler's Law   45

8   On Scientific Writing   57

9   How to Pass Examinations in Economics   63

10 The Alarming Cost of Model Changes:
      A CASE STUDY   69

11 Elementary Economic Education   73

12 The Intellectual and the Market Place   85

FOREWORD

THIS VOLUME came into being largely through the efforts of the author's colleagues at the Graduate School of Business of the University of Chicago, where George Stigler is Charles R. Walgreen Distinguished Service Professor of American Institutions. We persuaded Professor Stigler that several of his talks and essays delivered to (or written for the edification of) relatively small groups belong to a larger audience.

I shall not recall here Mr. Stigler's already well-known accomplishments in the two worlds of which he writes—the economic and the academic—nor his parallel achievements as a writer and a lecturer. I shall merely note that his eminence in any of these four specialties, in a demonstration of Stigler's own Rule of Multiple Specialization (see page 11), is readily acknowledged by his colleagues in the other three.

Beyond this, I commend the reader to Mr. Stigler's spare but unsparing prose while sounding a warning. As you stroll through these pages, tread cautiously. The path is strewn with sharp insights and prickly facts.

GEORGE P. SHULTZ, Dean
Graduate School of Business
University of Chicago

ix

Part One

MOSTLY ABOUT
UNIVERSITIES

This account of academic reform appeared in the Bulletin of the American Association of University Professors, Winter 1947. I could vouch for its authenticity.

1

An Academic Episode

I HAD been proposing a favorite thesis that our universities are run in reverse. While a man is still young and energetic and curious, he is required to teach so many elementary courses and read so many examinations—and scrub so many floors at home—that he can do no research. Even his summers must be spent earning more money. When he gets older, his teaching load is cut in half and his paper work is delegated to assistants—and his salary doubles. But now he is usually beyond creative work, and develops his bridge or golf. Pinzio, the venerable head of romance languages, agreed that there was much truth in the indictment, but thought that any remedy would be worse than the disease. He related the following story.

About thirty years ago a young man named Seguira

became the rector of a university in a South American country in which his father had recently financed a successful revolution. Seguira, who previously had been quite the gay young blade, surprised everyone when he immediately settled down to become a serious-minded reformer—a sort of Latin Hutchins. He began casting about for reform, of which—Pinzio said—the university could stand a good deal, and eventually hit upon the merit system. He soon issued the following regulations.

In June of each year any member of the faculty could challenge the person immediately above him in rank to a competitive examination. The examination was to be made out and graded by a group of impartial professors in the United States. (Seguira told Pinzio that this country was chosen to make bribery more expensive.) If the challenger won, he exchanged position and salary with his former superior. Thus an able graduate student could in successive years become an instructor, an assistant professor, an associate professor, and a professor.

There was a terrible uproar, and some shrill glee, when this announcement came out. Some of the older men were very bitter, and emphasized the fact that the rectorship was not included in the competition. But most of the younger men were delighted at the prospect, Pinzio among them.

The announcement was made in September, and some very desirable effects were observed during the first year. The physicist Antonio bought a new pair of spectacles so he could once again read small print. Cardan, the economist who had been spending most of his time running a noodle factory, engaged an assistant professor (who could not challenge him for two years) to tutor him in the developments in economics during the previous fifteen years. The senior professor in chemistry announced in December, once he fully understood the plan, that for reasons of health he was retiring the next June, and several others followed him. The library experienced an unprecedented rush. Learned journals—especially American—came out of dusty stacks, and hot disputes raged over the attempts of some men to draw out all of the modern treatises in a field. This, indeed, was the one clear disadvantage of the reform: men began to hoard knowledge. Few were willing to discuss their field except with better-informed people, and the exceptions were attributed to deceit as often as to arrogance. The graduate students suffered most: Filipo devoted his year course in the advanced theory of functions to a review of Euclid; Danto succeeded in getting many economics students to read Alfred instead of Adam Smith; and Ricard reviewed the Baconian theory, in painstaking detail, in his course on Shakespeare.

Yet the results of the competitions the following June were generally conceded to be beneficial. Several men began rapid, if overdue, movement toward retirement. Rumor had it that the unsuccessful and incompetent associate professor Jordon, whose wife was the daughter of the chairman of his department, was contemplating divorce. Pinzio became an associate professor.

SEGUIRA in particular was delighted with the outcome. But he was worried by the tendency of teachers to devote their graduate courses to empty and irrelevant subjects; so he amended the regulations to grant five points (in a hundred) to a teacher for each of his students who won a challenge. This new rule led to careful calculation: would five points outweigh a superior performance by the student in the examination? The general belief was that professors gained, and assistant professors lost, by careful instruction. The scheme led to some paradoxes the following year: Dourni was challenged by seven of his graduate students and all got higher grades in the examination, but his thirty-five point bonus kept his position for him.

By the next autumn another unanticipated result of the reform became apparent. There was a precipitous fall in enrollments of graduate students, and it was soon discovered that all who could afford it had gone to the United States for graduate work. Seguira shared the professors' indignation at this maneuver, and vowed to amend the regulations the following spring. But meanwhile a heavy gloom settled on the staff: were not the migratory students virtually studying the examination questions?

The gloom was justified by the fact. Of the sixty-one students who spent the year in the United States, forty-six won their challenge the following spring. Nor were the results so generally approved as the year before. It is true that several fossils continued their steady march to the museum, and several able young men moved up another rank (Pinzio among them). But Storeo, the brilliant young astronomer, was defeated by a mediocre graduate student who—with the examiner—had spent the year studying some obscure variable stars. And Birnii fell because his magisterial command of political theory did not extend to the details of the New England township.

Seguira was in a quandary. To rule out migration was to invite charges of provincialism and inbreeding; to permit it on the current scale was to destroy graduate study. He finally devised a compromise: the examinations would be given by professors chosen at random from the United States, England, France, Sweden, and Germany. Now if a graduate student went abroad, four times out of five he would guess the wrong country. The amendment did stop the mass migration, but it had its own embarrassments: one

4

sociologist had the same examination question, by chance, in two consecutive years, and each time gave the same answer. The first year he received an ignominious flunk (from Stockholm), and the second year he was offered a professorship (at Harvard).

And as the scheme entered its third year, a further effect could no longer be overlooked. Research had almost stopped. Once observed, of course, it was easy to explain. A man was likely to pass the examination with high marks if he knew what others were doing; it did not help his chances materially to do something himself. The faculty was becoming extremely well-read, and extremely unenterprising. The most prominent exceptions showed the advisability of the rule. Therespi had continued his careful researches on the fruit fly and lost in two challenges. Laboro had finished the seventh volume of his monumental history of South America, and flunked the question on the Crusades.

Another year and some serious faculty losses were required to arouse Seguira to the importance of this problem. Once persuaded, he issued still another amendment: a man was to receive two points for each article, and seven for each book. He wanted to restrict these bonuses only to current publications, but the opposition was too strong. Even the younger men, especially the successful younger men, were complaining of the baneful effects of insecurity of tenure. And it was pointed out that definitive works required time—perhaps even two years. Seguira compromised by including publications since a date ten years in the past.

The calculations of the faculty now became even more complex. A book (seven points), or the training of a superior student (five points)? The writing of the book might require three years, but the points were received every year thereafter, whereas the student might eventually leave. The answers at which the faculty finally arrived were various.

5

Cimoor, whose father owned a publishing house, succeeded in getting out two books within the first year, and so influential was his father that many of the reviews were neutral. The political scientist Broze withdrew a book already in page proof, and published the nineteen chapters as nineteen articles. This, however, occasioned less complaint than Cardan's publication of a book of readings. But still, research revived somewhat.

THIS SEQUENCE of felt difficulty and hopeful amendment, Pinzio said, might have gone on as indefinitely as the unstable political foundations of Seguira's position permitted, had not two developments come to pass. The first was the sudden dawning on Seguira that this patchwork of rules was gradually obliterating the whole purpose of his reforms. This was brought home when, in the next annual competition, four professors came out of unwilling retirement and three, with the aid of their writings of previous years, began again to climb the academic ladder. This particular development, of course, could be dealt with through a new rule —but where was it leading?

The conjunction of the second event proved decisive. Shortly after this awakening, Seguira received an invitation from the towering University of South America to become its rector. The regents wrote that his reputation for originality and enterprise was international, and that the success of his experiments indicated the need for a wider field of application. He accepted the new position, as much as a refuge as a promotion.

And what happened to Seguira? we demanded, and to the university? Seguira became as conservative as his reputation would allow, Pinzio assured us. And the merit system? Only one more amendment was added: a man could receive a permanent bonus of any number of points the department chairman deemed fit, when an offer was received from another university.

This is the only brave piece in the volume: to defend specialism in academic life ranks just above defense of racial prejudice. It appeared in the Bulletin of the American Association of University Professors, Winter 1951-52.

2

Specialism: A Dissenting Opinion

ONE SUBJECT on which almost all academic specialists agree is the evils of specialism. My university and many others impose courses in contemporary civilization or general science on the students to give them a well-rounded view of the universe. The view certainly will not have many edges when economics is taught by historians, and psychology is taught by economists. My university and many others contrive interdepartmental seminars to integrate the allied sciences and to explore some subject to its ultimate reaches. Some of these research teams have pushed so far that rescue parties will soon be necessary.

Specialism (like its cousin, the younger generation) would probably be mostly something to be deplored when one is in a nostalgic mood, were it not for the educational foundations. For their priests, "the integration of knowledge" is the cry to perpetual battle with the sinning specialists. To them we owe (and are still paying for) some of the shiny ornaments of our intellectual life—the institute that "cuts across conventional lines" and the interdisciplinary project.

It is my thesis that this worship of the cosmopolitan mind is romantic foolishness. As a gesture toward consistency, I shall illustrate my arguments in support of this position from the field of economics rather than attempt to glean a variety of examples from other disciplines of which I lack a thorough (specialized) knowledge. Out of consideration for noneconomists, however, I shall take my illustrations from "general" economics rather than from my own field of specialization (homogeneous oligopoly).

The Division of Labor

ONE MAN working alone can make perhaps 20 pins in a day. If the task is divided among 10 men, each of whom specializes in doing a part of the work, they can make 48,000 pins each day, or 4,800 pins per man. With this famous example Adam Smith put the division of labor among the great organizing principles of social activity, and for two centuries or more men have prospered by pushing the principle into every nook of economic life and also into every nook of intellectual life. It is essential for the young scholar to specialize: only in this way can he acquire more knowledge than his older and more experienced colleagues. Indeed, for both the young and the old scholar there are only two defenses against the accumulation of knowledge: generalization and specialization, and of these the latter is more efficient.

For example, Wesley C. Mitchell specialized in the

study of business cycles and extended our knowledge much beyond that of his predecessors; now many specialists are studying the cycles in particular industries or economic processes, and are adding greatly to the knowledge Mitchell accumulated. Again, thirty years ago men began to estimate national income. The precision and detail of these estimates have increased continuously as men specialized in estimating particular components of the national income, such as incomes of independent professional men and incomes of financial institutions.

This is as trite as water: specialism is the royal road to efficiency in intellectual as in economic life. The widely trained individual simply cannot hold his own in any field with the individual of equal ability and energy who specializes in that field. Indeed, the individual who now attempts to survey a whole science or discipline is viewed as a popularizer ("journalist") or even as a charlatan, but definitely not as a creative scholar. It is notorious that when a man combines two diverse specialties, the members of each specialty acknowledge the man's eminence only in the specialty with which they are unfamiliar.

What Division Points?

EVERY SPECIALIST will admit the advantages of the division of labor. Since the modern specialist is equal in capacity to the less specialized scholar of former days, and only slightly more neurotic, it follows that the former knows more about that in which he specializes. But, it is said, many problems cross the boundaries that separate specialties, and they cannot be dealt with satisfactorily unless the specialist follows them, and this he is not able to do. In a more radical version, it is said that most problems of importance must be treated as wholes—the sum is more than the parts

—and true understanding cannot be reached by any number of specialists.

Such remarks almost always rest on one or both of two propositions. First, that most real problems cross the boundaries of the specialties, *i.e.*, the specialties are wrongly defined. Second, that all specialists of a given genre have the same knowledge and competence. Both of these propositions are wholly wrong.

The border "lines" of specialties are really zones, but let us ignore this for a moment. It should be obvious that the lines of division between specialties arose out of experience. No congress of academicians drew up the present lines of division. Instead, these lines of division developed pragmatically because they proved tenable and useful limits at which the investigation of considerable sets of important problems could be dropped without vitiating the results.

The economists, for example, rid themselves of psychology because they found that they could construct a body of theory that could deal with a wide set of important problems and yield useful predictions, without building on a complicated theory of individual behavior. They rid themselves, at least for a time, of political science, because in the contemporary private enterprise economy they were analyzing, the state played a relatively minor and unpervasive rôle.

Nor are these lines of division among specialists immutably fixed. They react to changes in the phenomena to be studied in the social sciences and they react to changes in the state of knowledge in all sciences. Specialists are continuously experimenting with new ranges of analysis to see if better understanding of their problems can be reached. It is a tribute to the significance of the current boundaries that most of these experiments are failures.

For example: Each decade, for nine decades, economists

have read widely in the then current psychological literature. These explorers have published their findings, and we
have found them wanting—wanting in useful hypotheses
about economic behavior that baffles us. Perhaps the next
effort will be successful, and then we shall quickly establish
a new specialty, *psychonomics*.

Nor are the specialists a set of experts cast in one mold.
No two of the creative minds in a discipline have the same
knowledge, techniques, or interests. Some economic theorists
are interested in the formal structure of the science, and
work in fields like the theory of games and dynamical systems. Other theorists are interested in the substantive elements of the science, and work in fields like input-output
analysis and the statistical analysis of demand. Some men
are learned in mathematics, others can understand income
tax returns, still others are students of the history of our
discipline.

It is a gross impertinence for an outsider to tell the
specialists that they do not know how to deal with the
problems on which they specialize. It is almost equally
impertinent, and no more helpful, to assert that the problems which are dealt with by specialists are less important
than other problems. Of course the "lines of division" between specialties may be inefficient at a given time, but
only by employing successfully a new range of analysis will
the inefficiency be demonstrated and located.

Teachers Are Different?

THE HARDY universalist may concede the greater efficiency of specialism and the fact that specialties are based
upon reason, but he will nevertheless say that teaching is
different. Specialism is good or at least a necessary evil in
research, but in the classroom we need more widely trained

individuals who can convey the essential unity of knowledge. I shall discuss this view only with respect to college education.

The good teacher is a mysterious person, and yet we must know his character before we can prescribe his training. In my view, the good teacher is not distinguished by the breadth of his knowledge, by the lucidity of his exposition, or by the immediate reactions of his students. His fundamental task is not to dispense information, for in this rôle he is incomparably inferior to the written word. His task is to fan the spark of genuine intellectual curiosity and to instill the conscience of a scholar—to communicate the enormous adventure and the knightly conduct in the quest for knowledge. (I realize that this view of the teacher's function will strike many as austere. They will emphasize the need for sympathetic development of the utmost in each individual, and turn teaching into coaching. I think they do a disservice to mediocre as well as to good minds.)

To this end, the fundamental requirements of the good teacher are competence—how can the incompetent be other than slovenly?—and intellectual vitality—how can the sedentary excite us to bold adventure?

These traits may be acquired by wide reading and deep reflection, without engaging in research and becoming a specialist. But it is an improbable event. It is improbable psychologically: it asks a man to have the energy to read widely and the intellectual power to think freshly, and yet to do no research. He is to acquire knowledge and construct ideas—and keep them a secret. It is improbable scientifically: it asks a man to be competent in his understanding of work that he has had no part in constructing. At least in economics this is almost impossible. There is no book that states the consensus of the profession on the ideas that are changing —and these are naturally the most interesting ideas. Only the man who has tried to improve the ideas will know their strengths and weaknesses. Scholarship is not a spectator sport.

And so, on my view of the good teacher, almost invariably he will engage in research, and if this research is to be professionally respectable, it must be specialized research. Then his standards of intellectual performance are maintained by the critical scrutiny of his fellow scholars. The teacher who does not publish must have the conscience of a saint if he is not to take things easy: to pontificate instead of to reason; to conjecture rather than to know. It is not good for a man to associate only with his inferiors, and students are vastly the teacher's inferior in prestige and status.

When the search for universalism goes so far that men teach outside their general area of competence, the results seem to me completely bad. The students are subjected to diffident reports on the reading of the teacher. The teacher is compelled to spend a huge amount of time acquiring even the minimum knowledge necessary to last out the class hour. He tires of saying that he does not know the answers to reasonable questions, and acquires the habit of making up answers, and the students come to believe that a nodding acquaintance with many subjects is the earmark of the educated man.

The Last Stand

EVEN THOSE who find the foregoing arguments convincing will refuse to welcome their message. Why do they cling to the goal of the universal mind?

Partly it is moon-reaching. It would indeed be fine to know many disciplines, I suppose, although heaven knows the ground shifts fast enough in debates even now. It would also be fine to have a salary of $24,000 a year, every six months.

Partly too, it is a humble confession of every man that he failed to learn many things he would now cherish, and feels that with a broader training these painful gaps in his knowledge would be smaller and (what is more doubtful) that he would still know all he does now of his specialty. Yet such gaps in knowledge are inevitable so long as men are free to change their interests and work, to say nothing of deficiencies of elementary and secondary education.

And partly, too, it is a recognition of the sad fact that the most consummate mastery of a specialty may not prevent a man from playing the fool in other areas. We hope that the lessons of logic and evidence are universal in their applicability, but they seem to have a tendency to stick to their subject matter. At least we find it all too easy to name specialists whose logical ability and standards of evidence collapse when they step outside their specialties. But this is a defect of the man, not of his training and work. He lacks a general intelligence even if he has a partial genius. Specialism does not cause his deficiency; rather it tends to restrict him to the area where the deficiency is not present.

Are we, then, to become a race of guilds? Are we to converse easily and fruitfully with our fellow specialists but to be overcome by gauche silences in our association with other kinds of specialists? We can easily avoid this outcome. Let us all specialize a little in one field—it does not matter whether it is romantic music or interplanetary communication or the fruit fly or judicial review. Then we shall have a common meeting ground on which to have the pleasant and profitable jousts of knowledge and wit, and on which we can form some estimate of the quality of a man. I leave to the specialists in social communication the selection of the precise field.

Of all the objectionable methods of persuasion, the use of false authority seems to me more immoral even than physical coercion. Hence the present piece, written in 1960, previously unpublished.

3

The National Commission as an Instrument of Controlled Impartiality

OF THE DOZENS upon dozens of governmental and private commissions, the most recent (as of December, 1960) to report was the National Goals Commission. Let us consider its membership:

Henry M. Wriston, *former President of Brown University,* CHAIRMAN

Frank Pace, Jr., *former Secretary of the Army, General Dynamics Corp.*

Erwin D. Conham, *editor, Christian Science Monitor*

James B. Conant, *former President of Harvard University*

Colgate W. Darden, Jr., *former Governor of Virginia, President of University of Virginia*

Crawford H. Greenewalt, *President, du Pont*

Alfred M. Gruenther, *President, American Red Cross*

Clark Kerr, *President, University of California*
James R. Killian, Jr., *Chairman, M.I.T.*
George Meany, *President, AFL-CIO*

It is at least a fair sample of the membership of national commissions: distinguished educators (possibly too many in this case), appropriately prominent business men and union officials, a representative or two of the huge nonprofit foundation industry, and a name or two from the fourth and other estates.

We might ask: why did not each of these men write his own set of goals for America? And why did not each of the several members of the Randall Commission tell us how to conduct our foreign economic policy? Why does not each of the numerous members of the National Monetary Commission give us his own ideas on a good monetary system? And similarly for the thirty members of the Rockefeller Brothers Fund, which has touched upon every aspect of our life.

The question is child-like in its simplicity; I doubt that the answers would share this simplicity. It will in high probability be said that each man's personal statement would not have the breadth of vision, or rest upon the variety of knowledge, the diversity of viewpoint, that the group as a whole possesses. Quite true, no doubt, and yet—what is the mysterious alchemy of committee proceedings that preserves each man's virtues, and weeds out each man's prejudices and blind spots?

There *is* such an alchemy in collaboration on technical matters: if a chemist and a lawyer collaborate on devising a chemical patent, the work is better than either could do because they have skills that supplement each other. But in the more conventional task of telling the nation what to do, there is no such expertise—almost everything basic is a question of judgment and of the values one places on high.

And in devising of policy, the commission seeks to do precisely the opposite of adding the special knowledge possessed by each member: it seeks the largest common denominator of all of their prejudices and interests. Any very extensive set of dissents will destroy any impact the report of the Commission will have—the reader will instinctively feel that if the Commission cannot convince itself of the wisdom of its views, no outsider should take it very seriously. Only a moderate amount of skilled dissent is tolerable.

There is one other inevitable force which helps a committee to get out a report: no man feels that it must represent exactly his own viewpoint. If he were so individualistic (and possibly egotistic) as to believe so, then he would never accept membership on a commission, except to sabotage it—and one such performance would be enough to take him off the eligible list.

I have made a very strong statement: *that a commission's report does not and cannot reflect the strengths of its individual members.* Let me illustrate it.

The Commission on National Goals is not very fair game becaue its task was inherently impossible. One example will suffice to reveal its stance. The Commission contained several experts on labor unions—practitioners such as George Meany and Crawford Greenewalt as well as a distinguished academic specialist, Clark Kerr. This is the sum total of their (and the other seven's) wisdom on this troubled area:

Collective bargaining between representatives of workers and employers should continue as the nation's chief method for determining wages and working conditions.

Conferences among management, union leaders, and representatives of the public can contribute to mutual understanding of problems that affect the welfare of the economy as a whole.

Corporations and labor unions must limit the influence they exert on the private lives of their members. Unions must continue to develop adequate grievance procedures and greater opportunities for legitimate opposition.

These generalities do not have the merit of being goals—everything is machinery—or of being correct (collective bargaining is much less important than competition in fixing wages and working conditions).

The Rockefeller Brothers Fund somehow enticed twenty distinguished individuals—this time very heavily loaded with academicians, but chaired by Nelson Rockefeller—also to tell us where and how to go. Its report, *The Challenge to America: Its Economic and Social Aspects*, provides innumerable examples of commissionese. One could spend a long time on its specific recommendations, of which my favorite is:

The present double standard of regulation as between common carriers on the one hand and contract and private carriers on the other is basically unsound and a single standard of regulation should be developed where possible.

This bold, nay, heroic, recommendation says we should extend or contract the regulation of motor trucking.

These examples could be multiplied, but not with profit. Committees are devices to keep individuals from going very wrong, not devices to reach truth where the policy issues are seriously controversial or the analytical or factual questions are complex. No commission has ever solved a hard problem in any intellectual sense: at its rare best, a commission has split or overawed the opposition.

Why, then, form commissions? And if they are formed, why not have each member state his own beliefs clearly and emphatically—letting the reader make for himself the synthesis which the committee's deliberations now seek to achieve?

The most important answer, I am convinced, is that the commission is deemed an efficient instrument of propaganda. The many semi-unanimous voices will somehow sound louder in chorus than the sum of their individual efforts.

The whole art of commissionmanship is to select honorable and disinterested members who will mostly agree with the position which the creators of the commission desire. This is not so difficult as it may sound, because most honorable and disinterested men of distinction [1] have no very definite ideas on most specific questions (in this they are no different from the rest of us), but [2] have definite, known sentiments and inclinations; and hence are predictable.

No one can create an impressive commission which will recommend that Castro be given Florida, but it would be easy to construct equally distinguished and impartial groups to recommend that future exploitation of atomic energy for peaceful uses be primarily public, or, if one wishes, primarily private. It would be just as easy to make up a fine commission to support, or oppose, an immensely expanded federal urban renewal program, or increased (or decreased) foreign aid, or, in fact, either side of any question that is really debatable in the near future. A good chairman and a good knowledge of the men who make up the slowly changing panel of eligible commission members are all that one needs.

Not all commissions are created primarily to propagandize particular policy views. Some are created only to buy time: a commission will surely take at least six months or a year to report, and meanwhile the passions or crisis which called it into existence may have subsided. And there are politicians and foundation heads—the only two respectable sources of large funds for public commissions—who are so naive as to believe that the commission is an appropriate instrument for uncovering truth; or confirming it. I suspect that this is the origin of the Goals Commission, as it was of the only one (the Attorney-General's National Committee for the Study of the Antitrust Laws—65 members) of which I was a member.

If the commissions are primarily propaganda instruments, why do the distinguished citizens join them, attend the meetings, thumb the reams of staff papers, and sign a document that most imperfectly represents their individual views? Simply because they too are propagandists. They will have signed a report that moderately misrepresents their views on ten questions, but their strongly held 11th position got in, or at least part way in. If they have no strong views, then they are simply propagandizing themselves—joining the public-spirited, enlightened leaders of the community, adding nice lines to their *Who's Who* entries.

Academicians have another reason for joining: not to displease the important persons, and in particular foundations, who push the commissions. The friendship of a foundation is second in importance only to a professor's professional reputation, and within considerable limits the friendship will be an adequate substitute for reputation.

I do not conclude that commissions would be excluded from the good society, and not only because this is so grave an issue that a commission should deal with it. Those commissions which buy time are often splendid social assets— they provide a cooling off period on public passions, a function the United States Senate no longer fulfills so efficiently. Those which propagandize—that is, most of the other commissions—are finding that competition, the life of trade, can become the death of influence. The commission reports are now so numerous as to have become unimportant. Yet they will undoubtedly persist, unless displaced by some more dramatic innovation such as the summit conference, until a fateful day. That day, the theory of probability tells us, must eventually come: *two* distinguished and impartial commissions will simultaneously issue conflicting reports. Then the secret will be out: bringing twenty men together for eighty hours yields a weak formulation of somebody's ideas.

This paper was written at the Center for Advanced Study in the Behavioral Sciences in 1958, where it received the Award of the Interdisciplinary Knot. Its characters have been thinly disguised for publication, except for my lamented friend Sidney Siegel. He would, I am sure, rather have one facet of a remarkable personality caricatured than be given flimsy anonymity.

4

Stigler's First Law of Sympathy

The Previous Literature

THE HEROIC figure in the scientific analysis of sympathy, before the appearance of the present essay, was Freud. Writing with incandescent intuition and a command of the literature that is fortunately uncommon, he addressed himself squarely to the central problem of this paper: the construction of a law of sympathy which describes precisely the relationship between the quantity of sympathy and the object of the sympathy.

This problem became, indeed, a fixation: Freud recurred to it in literally a score of his lesser known essays, seeking by an immensely resourceful panoply of methodologies to demonstrate the existence of such a law. We must attach the heaviest significance to his final, definitive, and lugubri-

I wish to express my debt to T............... P............... for performing on his abacus the tedious statistical calculations, and to John Thukey for challenging their accuracy.

ous assessment of the prospects for finding such a law: *Es ist ganz unmöglich.*[1]

The famous intradisciplinary research team, known as Arroh-Friedmon-Reader-Soloh, has recently renewed the attack upon this problem, employing the most powerful techniques of modern mathematical economics, including ridicule, only to reach the same conclusion as Sam Freud. Their results culminated in what they termed the AFRS Theorem:

If S is sympathy, and RS is any regularity in the behavior of S, then RS is topologically indifferent.

But the team, as its last joint act, has since repudiated this theorem,[2] and now three much weaker propositions have been offered in its stead, each an individual effort:

Proposition A: If S is sympathy, S belongs to A.

Proposition F: Scientific laws are provided at minimum cost in optimum quantity by a well organized price system.

Proposition S: Sympathy is not a durable commodity.

Only Proposition F calls for brief, and cavalier, comment.

Friedmon offers (without price) three arguments in defense of the proposition that the offer of an adequate sum for a law of sympathy would have called forth such a law, if one existed. His first proof is that potato chips are supplied in this manner; this proof fails because potato chips are different from sympathy. His second proof is that the Russians, who do not have a well organized price system, have

1. "Schrecklichkeit Noch Einmal," *Gesammelte Schriften*, xiv, 27.
2. One member, who prefers to remain anonymous writes: "My . . . colleagues have slopped again, and I would appreciate it if you would refer, not to the AFRS Theorem, but to the AFS Fallacy."

no law of sympathy; this proof fails because he cannot read Russian. His final proof, if such it may be called, is that competition always works well, and scholars are competitive; but he forgets—although for him this must have been especially difficult—that not all scholars work.

The most recent work in this tradition has been done by the experimentalist, Sidney Siegel, PH.D.[3] Siegel produced suitable objects of sympathy under laboratory conditions and then measured the amount of sympathy they elicited. The objects of sympathy were a set of students who were subjected to tortures ranging from a hot foot to what the experimentalist describes as "scenes difficult to view with composure even before the next of kin arrived." As the measure of sympathy, each observer was asked to draw a coin from one of three buckets. These buckets contained pennies, nickels, and $20 gold pieces, and the observer was asked to withdraw a coin proportional to the sympathy he felt for the student in the iron cage. Siegel found that sympathy is always at a maximum: whether the observer was laughing callously or sobbing in utter misery, he or she always withdrew a $20 gold piece, which under the conditions of the experiment he or she was entitled to keep.

Siegel's demonstration that sympathy is always at a maximum is structured, and therefore well worth the $13 million in $20 gold pieces his study cost the Ford Foundation. But this usually careful experimentalist had one crucial flaw in his design, which vitiates the results: the bucket with the $20 gold pieces had better illumination. One may also raise a question, or at least an eyebrow, at his collection of observers for the experiments: it is surely remarkable that under random sampling with replacement the observers were: Henry Siegel (100 times), Horace Siegel (50 times),

3. In *The Uses of Stanford Graduate Students.*

27

Hortense Siegel (700 times), and Mrs. Sidney Siegel (re-mainder of times).[4]

Genesis of My First Law[5]

I CUSTOMARILY begin the day at a sedentary pace. After an ice cold shower for twenty minutes, I get out of bed and read one of the New York *Times* Hundred Neediest Cases to maintain a sense of well-being. I then eat a light breakfast and compose a stanza of my romantic epic, *Science is a Boy's Best Friend.*

But things were very different on April 11, 1946. For one thing I had not gotten to bed the previous night, and so did not have to arise. For another, I was in a railroad station. And for still another, I was feeling sorry for myself —a fugitive sentiment due to acute financial distress, a sick child, a threatening letter from my wife in Reno, and a grand jury indictment. And then it happened, a characteristic instance of serendipity. My sympathy for myself, I carelessly calculated, was at the rate of 127 units per minute, and the vagrant thought flitted through my mind: how sorry was I for other people? I was about to dismiss the query with an off-hand "enough," when it occurred to me that my sympathy for a person fell off, the more distant he was. And he could be far away not only in a geographical sense, but also socially. Would it not be possible to construct a vast social law corresponding to Newton's law for physical bodies, but naturally superior because distance was a more complex concept in social relations?

4. In a recent letter from the French Riviera, Siegel's secretary writes: "M. Siegel now believes his table of random numbers contained misprints."
5. I describe the discovery only as a contribution to the sociology of science. Hasty readers may prefer to skip this section, and careful readers to go back to the first section. I am indebted to Kenneth Burke for writing between the lines.

I kept putting this line of thought out of mind, but finally the handsome young lady on the bench facing me got her stocking straightened and I recurred to it. Its plausibility mounted, and I vowed to dedicate my time and talents to its development.

For several years I worked with a zeal, tenacity, and resourcefulness that modesty will not allow me to describe. And to no avail. The shrewdest hypothesis was contradicted by evidence; the most brilliant conjecture crashed upon the shoal of inconsistency. I grew sorrier for myself, and at one point my self-sympathy attained the rate of 197 units per minute.

In the fall of 1950 the outlook was so bleak that I contemplated abandonment of the scholarly life for that of the concert violinist. A chance encounter with a Frank Reach did much to end this sterile period. We met in a Sausalito bar, and I eagerly poured my tale of woe into his receptive ear. His initially cheerful, not to say flushed, countenance turned somber and finally despondent, and he suggested that we both consult a psychiatrist. He had heard of a Dr. Samage, unusual among his craft in possessing a two-person couch. I remember little of the session—the damp weather had forced Frank and me to take preventive ministrations against pneumonia—except that Dr. Samage's second question (his first concerned financial resources) was directed to Frank, and asked for a recounting of the occasions on which the subject of sex had entered his head. In all candor, Frank appeared to have a one-track mind.

The next day I was the subject of analysis, and as I recall, the conversation went as follows:

Dr.: What's eating you, chum?

I: Misfortune is my mistress.

[To be continued, perhaps, in a future year.]

About a decade ago I started to review a Festschrift, one, as I recall, seeking to honor a famous continental economist. This is what came out, and was rejected by the Journal of Political Economy. It is printed in its entirety.

5

Festschriften

"PROFESSOR Ausgeschrieben," I said, "I promised to contribute an article to the Festschrift for Professor Geplänkel —he once got me an offer from Chicarvard and I felt I owed it to him. But time has slipped by, and here I am three weeks from the deadline without an idea."

Ausgeschrieben partially opened one eye, but the lid quickly fell back into place. "Giorgio," he replied, "it is simple. Have you a good article on hand? No? An article? No? A rejected article? No? Lucky. Then take one of the old ones —say that one on what Pascal would have thought of indifference curves—and do it over with a few nice references to Geplänkel's *Eléments d'économie symmetrique*."

This sounded too simple, and a trifle jaded. So I drifted over to Ballpoint (14 Festschrift contributions). Ballpoint

31

was, as usual, on the ball and to the point. "Take that idea you've been peddling at lunch, that only by eliminating marriage can we recruit a sufficient number of good elementary teachers, surround it with statistics, and send it in." This was good advice, and Ballpoint had used it often, but I simply cannot inflate a random idea into a purposive paper.

So I sought out Zweistein: "Geplänkel isn't a bad man, even considering that 1936 article on the artichoke cartel, and a Festschrift can be justified. The Festschrift honors him not only by its existence but also by the unfavorable comparison it makes with his work. So don't take this too seriously: Do the best that circumstances permit and remember that no one will buy the book."

I sat down and began to write: "The celebrated Pascal, it is true, never wrote on indifference curves. Yet if one interprets his work with the aid of Geplänkel's profound schemata, there emerges a picture. . . ."

This speech was given at the annual Trustee dinner of the University of Chicago in 1962. It reveals secrets on how to create a great university, but not our secret of how to get people really to want one.

6

Meager Means and Noble Ends

I PROPOSE tonight to look at higher education through the morbid eyes of an economist. The economic side of education is not the most interesting side even to an economist, but it is sufficiently important to invite at least a modest survey.

Higher education is a competitive industry—a large, reasonably prosperous competitive industry. Competitive industries display characteristic forms of behavior which I hope my fellow economists will allow me to simplify into a set of rules. Though most of these rules are not essential to reach the conclusions about the future of this university at which I am aiming, let me state several and indicate their applicability to higher education, if only to persuade you that you are in fact in a competitive industry.

First, it is a well-known rule that an increase in the demand for the product of a large competitive industry will produce a rise in its price unless the industry's technology is improving apace. I think it is fair to say that the technology of college teaching is not among the most dynamic branches of modern life. The last really notable advance in college teaching in recent times was the invention of the printing press. I find it suggestive of the pleasant stability of our teaching ways that it is being hailed as a major advance that books are now sold without bindings. Meanwhile the growth of the number of students has been immense, and—to use Chicago as an example—tuition, which is our price, has risen from $120 in 1895 to $1450 next year (1963), an average of about 4 per cent a year.

Second, if an industry's demand is growing rapidly, new firms will enter the industry on a large scale. Here again our colleges and universities fit the rule: in 1760 there were 6 colleges, or 1 for every 300,000 of population; in 1960 there were 1,400 odd colleges and universities, or 1 for every 130,000 of population. I have excluded normal schools and junior colleges from this count of schools, or the ratio would be 1 for every 90,000 of population. Enrollments have risen faster than the number of schools, of course, so we have been moving away from, not toward, that professor on a short log facing one student. I am reminded of a remark once made by a colleague at Brown University, that after 30 years of teaching he had concluded that it would be just as effective to sit on the student and talk to the log.

There are many more of these rules for competitive industries. One rule says that large industries will solicit a variety of favors from the state—tariffs, subsidies, preferential tax status, and what not. Our colleges excel in this activity: I believe that higher education is the only industry whose customers are housed at the expense of the federal government, and the only industry whose employees are provided with frequent, extended vacations abroad. Then there is the rule that as the individual enterprise grows, it uses more and heavier machinery, but let us not tax, or Sol Tax, deans and vice presidents. There is the rule that employees with seniority will seek to devise working rules that reduce to a tolerable level the strains of a rigorous occupation; in our industry this is described as getting time off for research.

I hope I have persuaded you that there is at least a family resemblance between higher education and other competitive industries. There are many differences between our industry that produces knowledge and those that produce commodities—and not all are favorable to the education industry. But I ask you only to accept the conclusion that the main forces of competition exert powerful and similar influences on all competitive industries. I wish to invoke now the rule in competitive industries which provides the theme of my remarks.

This rule is, in the words of the discoverer, that the division of labor is limited by the extent of the market. If Adam Smith were alive tonight, he would no doubt be here, for his scientific genius would have overshadowed, for the Department of Economics, his regrettably conservative tendencies. I should assure him that his rule has been one of great power and fertility in economic theory. Although the rule has wider scope, for our purposes it is a sufficiently extended interpretation to state that the specialization of industries, of the plants within industries, and of the laborers within plants, all increase as an industry grows.

That there has been a continuous increase in the specialization of college teachers and researchers is a notorious fact, which I may illustrate within my craft. Adam Smith was first appointed the Professor of Logic at the University of Glasgow in 1751. Delayed by commitments at Edinburgh, he was substituted for by the Professor of Jurisprudence. On arriving at Glasgow he in turn substituted for the ailing professor of Moral Philosophy, whom he soon succeeded, and taught jurisprudence, politics, rhetoric, and belles-lettres. His lectures embraced natural theology, ethics, the history of civil society, tastes, and the history of philosophy, as well as containing some allusions to political economy. Today a professor of economics who pretended to be an expert in such far flung fields as international trade and retail trade, or economic history and the history of economics, would be branded a charlatan. All this is trite, and I shall not pursue it beyond remarking that in a group this large there may even be two or three people who share my belief that this increase in specialization is desirable as well as inevitable.

When specialization is suggested for institutions of higher education, however, one flies in the face of the announced goal of every respectable college and university. Every school, be it major, minor, or diminished seventh, desires to be strong in *every* significant scholarly discipline —certainly in the traditional arts and sciences. The specialized institutions themselves are ashamed of the fact, and the institutes for mechanics, such as M.I.T., boast of their growing strength in the social sciences and humanities. The university world says, with a singularly unanimous voice: let Cornell have hotel management, even let Washington have early Chinese literature; but Chicago, and Harvard, and Columbia, and Berkeley, and North-by-Northeast Methodist *must* be of the first rank in each of the basic sciences and humanities.

Rules are rules, and wishes are wishes. The wish of universal excellence is impossible to achieve. We cannot build plane triangles whose angles sum to 190°, nor universities which are uniformly excellent. Rather than treat this conclusion as a corollary, which would save me some trouble and you some time, I shall seek to establish it directly on the basis of two empirical propositions.

The first proposition is that there are at most fourteen really first class men in any field, and more commonly there are about six. Where, you ask, did I get these numbers? I consider your question irrelevant, but I shall pause to notice the related question: is the proposition true? And here I ask you to do some homework: gather with your colleagues and make up a numbered list of the twenty-five best men in one of your fields—and remember that these fields are specialized. Would your department be first class if it began its staffing in each field with the 25th or even the 15th, name? You have in fact done this work in appointment committees. I remember no cases of an embarrassment of riches, and I remember many where finding five names involved a shift to "promising young men," not all of whom keep their promises. I leave it to the professors of moral philosophy and of genetics to tell us whether the paucity of first class men is a sort of scientific myopia, a love of invidious ranking, or a harsh outcome of improvident marriages. But the proposition is true.

My second proposition is that no one school has much in the way of financial resources. Let us measure the wealth of a school by the amount it spends on faculty salaries—this payroll is its effective demand for professors. Like all simple numbers this wages-fund is not an ideal measure because a school's payroll would probably change in interesting ways if it decided to hire fewer and better men, but it is a sufficiently appropriate measure of buying power in the market for talented men. Then it is approximately true that the University of Chicago, with an academic wages-fund of $11,000,000 last year, had about one-third of 1 per cent of the total wages-fund of American universities and colleges, and perhaps 2 or 2.5 per cent of the wages-fund of the 50 largest universities. The richest of these fifty schools was probably Berkeley, with a wages-fund of $25,000,000, or 5 per cent of the total of the elite; Harvard had about $20,000,000; the University of Illinois, $17,000,000; Yale and Louisiana State University, each $7,500,000.

No school, not even the richest, has a wages-fund sufficient to hire one of the six best men in each field within the traditional arts and sciences. Fifty or a hundred institutions seriously seek such men, and even the fiftieth in wealth —which is about one-fourth as rich as the first in wealth— can bid enough for one or two such leaders to make them prohibitively expensive to others. The richest museum cannot acquire all the Rembrandts, and the richest school cannot hire all the leaders.

The basic trends of our time are strengthening the forces of diffusion of able men among institutions. The state has taxed away great private fortunes and generously supported public institutions. I have no doubt whatever that direct governmental subsidies to education will develop quota systems calculated to insure that each area and institution gets its share of the subsidies. The universally premier institution is becoming increasingly more unattainable. And the rules of economics make no exception for Chicago.

Economics is sometimes called the dismal science. I resent the phrase, for only young children should get angry at a corpus of knowledge that prevents hopeless but costly endeavors. To recognize a problem is to be better armed for rational actions, and I would now turn briefly to the actions I believe rational with the growth of specialization.

Universities will make their peace with the forces of specialization by a choice that falls somewhere between two poles: a universal mediocrity, at one end; a select and none too lengthy list of truly distinguished departments, on the other. I diffidently interpret the tradition of Chicago to be that which I also desire: the preservation of preeminence in a dozen of the most durable and basic disciplines, with at least respectable competence in the remainder of the basic disciplines—and nothing more.

I need not argue for such a preference here, because quite frankly none of you has the courage to oppose it. No one, indeed, seems to have the courage to defend mediocrity in any human activity; we are all hopeless romantics in the face of the naked fact that mediocrity is a fairly high estate —beyond the reach of a third of America's colleges and universities. Some people might quarrel with the limitation of my hopes, and tell me that in their field there are 1400 leaders, one for each college and university. Some people might say that all Chicago has to do—a phrase which in this context means that all Chancellor of the Exchequer George Beadle has to do—is to increase our endowment to, say, $10 billion dollars, next year. But I refuse to attribute these absurd views to a single one of you; the most meager compliment I can pay you is to assume that you accept the goal of selective eminence in light of the facts of competition.

Here I must pause to notice an objection, not to the goal of selective eminence, but to the view that it can consist of a scattering of distinguished departments throughout the university. It will be argued strongly by some men that this view of scattered excellence does not give due weight to the importance of cooperation between related fields— what the economist with his customary felicity calls complementarity. They will say that it is idle to speak of the possibility of outstanding departments of, say, physics and geophysics if chemistry and mathematics are weak; that an outstanding economics department requires outstanding history, political science, sociology, and statistics departments, and so on.

If this position is correct—if one department of a division can be eminent only on the condition that the other departments also are—then a very radical implication must be drawn. For this emphasis on complementarity does nothing to increase either the number of leaders in each field or the resources of a university. The implication must then be, quite simply, that selective eminence is still essential but must be achieved by making one division of the university—be it humanities, physical sciences, biological sciences, social sciences, or what not—and only this one division eminent, letting the remainder drift into respectable obscurity and possibly eventual oblivion.

I myself am sceptical that the complementarity of disciplines is this intimate and pervasive. There is no historical support for the view that the strength and achievements of any one social science depend intimately on the quality of the related social scientists—indeed I know no evidence for this view even when one enlarges his vision from a single institution to the world of scholarship. Economics, for example, has had two golden ages in the last century, from 1870 to 1900, and from 1935 to 1950, in the latter case with time out for a war. None of the other social sciences contributed importantly to either of these periods of sustained creativity. It will take heavy argument to convince me that the situation is radically different in the other divisions.

Mind you, no one will argue that able colleagues in other disciplines are not of value. Of course they are valuable to the specialist. Even if they were not available, it certainly would be impossible to get along without their books—but I shall not digress to examine the disquieting thought that perhaps it is the library that is keeping us together. What I do say, and earnestly believe, is that the dependence between disciplines is not so intimate that it must be maintained day by day within a single quadrangle. Until this is shown to be generally the case, I shall continue to believe that it is possible for an eminent university, and not just an eminent division, to exist.

One does not implement the goal of selective eminence for a university by telling some departments that they have been chosen for eminence and others that they have been condemned to respectability. There is room for chance, and the identity of the eminent departments will change slowly over time. There is more room for bold and gifted leadership, and it is a major attainable achievement to add two more to our preeminent departments.

But the goal of selective eminence cannot be pursued effectively if one ignores its selectivity. The goal cannot be achieved if we fail to be ruthless with proposals to increase our comprehensiveness: it is a fact of life that a vote for a school of journalism or an institute of automation is a vote to get rid of one or two first class men in physics or anthropology or law. The goal cannot be achieved if we insist that every department be *almost* preeminent: a vote to hire two expensive number twenty men is a vote to be rid of a number one man. These are different ways of saying that we must steer the difficult course between easy achievement and romantic impossibility. Some women are not fastidious and others insist upon marrying only perfect men. I know Chicago will not become a harlot; I do not want it to become a spinster.

I would add a word concerning a very troublesome lot who insist upon intruding into the discussions of their betters —I refer to the students. The student cannot achieve the best possible instruction in every specialized field at any one institution—this I shall now treat as a corollary. Though he does not study every specialized field even within one department, he would often profit by dividing his time between institutions whose strengths complement one another. There would be much merit in the development, at the graduate level, of the practice of spending a half year or a year at a second institution. This practice, you will recall, was prevalent during the fourteenth century, and on balance transportation has improved since then, aside from parking. The student would also gain perspective by living for a time in a different intellectual atmosphere, and the professors— for whom things must be good if they are to be good for the country—would also gain by the diversity of students.

The competitive industry is not one for lazy or confused or inefficient men: they will watch their customers vanish, their best employees migrate, their assets dissipate. It is a splendid place for men of force: it rewards both hard work and genius, and it rewards on a fine, generous scale. The success of a competitive enterprise is not in the least uncertain if its employees are able and diligent and its leadership sane and courageous. No such guarantees of success are present for a monopolist: he is overwhelmingly dominated by forces over which he has negligible control. This paradox that power deprives one of the certainty of success is partly verbal, as all good paradoxes are, but it contains an important truth.

I rejoice, therefore, not as an economist but as an employee of a singularly successful young competitive firm, in our troubles. If money came only to those who already had it, we should never have existed. If great schools could easily get and retain all the able men, Chicago would never have been worth mentioning. If we dwelled in a pastoral college village, where neither squalor nor crime had ever been observed, it is likely also that intellectual ferment and adventure would be absent. I shall not allow rhetoric to carry me to the absurdity of saying that only severe hardship allows of progress. I do say that if we wish, we can become the most successful firm in the industry, in fifteen major product lines.

Part Two

ALL ABOUT ECONOMICS

The reason this piece was not published when it was written (in 1948) is that too many readers found it persuasive. Time and events have probably not affected its truth.

7

Stigler's Law

I PROPOSE the following theorem, which (I hope) is sufficiently significant in its implications and rigorous in its demonstration to deserve the title of law:

> All Demand Curves are Inelastic, and
> All Supply Curves are Inelastic Too.

I have ventured to attach my name to this law because this will be its first completely explicit formulation and demonstration, although it has long lurked in the background of economic discussion. Both empirical and a priori demonstrations will be given.

Empirical Demonstration

IN PRINCIPLE it is impossible to establish empirically that all of the demand and supply curves that have ever existed or will someday exist are inelastic. Yet it is possible to establish a strong presumption that this is true by showing that, in a wide variety of investigations, elastic functions are conspicuous by their absence.

I begin with academic investigations, and necessarily my list of examples is insultingly incomplete, because editors' demands for brevity are also inelastic. First I shall report a few statistical findings; these deserve little weight because (aside from many technical weaknesses) almost always only short run functions are derived:

HENRY SCHULTZ:

With the possible exception of buckwheat (first and third periods), and of rye for the third period, the demand for all the ten commodities [sugar, corn, cotton, hay, wheat, potatoes, oats, barley, rye, and buckwheat] is inelastic (i.e., $/\eta/ < 1$). (*Theory and Measurement of Demand, p. 556.*)

DAVID A. WELLS:

A further analysis of the experiences of the New York and Brooklyn Bridge since its construction also reveals some curious tendencies of the American people in respect to consumption and expenditures. . . . In the third year, with a reduction of foot-fares to one-fifth of a cent [from one cent], the number of foot-passengers declined 440,395, or to an aggregate of 3,239,337; while the number of car-passengers (with a reduction of fare from five to two and a half cents) increased 10,130,957, or to 21,843,250. (*Recent Economic Changes, pp. 386-7.*)

46

E. H. SCHOENBERG:

. . . the coefficient of elasticity [of demand for cigarettes] at the means is —0.68. ("The Demand Curve for Cigarettes," *Journal of Business*, VI [1933], 35.)

E. J. BROSTER:

. . . the elasticities of demand for tea are 0.554 with respect to price and 0.284 with respect to income. ("Elasticities of Demand for Tea and Price-Fixing Policy," *Review of Economic Studies*, June, 1939, *p. 169*.)

R. M. WALSH:

The elasticity of supply for cotton acreage varied from 0.1 to 0.3 at different levels of price. ("Response to Price in Production of Cotton and Cottonseed," *Journal of Farm Economics*, XXVI [1944], 372.)

Much weightier is the testimony of economists who eschew mechanical calculation and carefully combine all the relevant information:

ALVIN H. HANSEN:

But most industries are confronted, at best, with a unit elasticity of demand. (*Fiscal Policy and Business Cycles, p. 326*.)

A. WALTERS:

Demand on the copper market has always been fairly inelastic; . . . ("The International Copper Cartel," *Southern Economic Journal*, XI [1944-45], 143.)

47

J. H. JONES:

If, however, we refer to the general demand [for coal] of the world as a whole, . . . it is undoubtedly true to say that it is inelastic. ("The Present Position of the British Coal Trade," *Journal of the Royal Statistical Society*, 1930, part I, *p. 10.*)

A. ABRAHAMSON:

High whiskey prices may have some slight effect in discouraging consumption; . . . (in *Price and Price Policies*, ed. W. Hamilton, *p. 427.*)

L. J. SELTZER:

The consumers' demand for credit is relatively insensitive to ordinary changes in interest rates, . . . ("Is a Rise in Interest Rates Desirable?" *American Economic Review*, December, 1945, *p. 837.*)

G. J. STIGLER:

One is struck by the narrow range of fluctuation of consumption, which certainly argues for an unusually inelastic demand [for wheat in the United Kingdom, 1890-1904]. ("Notes on the History of the Giffen Paradox," *Journal of Political Economy*, April, 1947, *pp. 154-5.*)

J. K. EASTMAN:

The demand for tin is highly inelastic over most of the price range experienced in recent years. . . . ("Rationalisation in the Tin Industry," *Review of Economic Studies*, October, 1936, *p. 13.*)

R. B. SHUMAN:

But within the usual experience range, there is no evidence that a shift of a few cents a gallon [of gasoline] has any material effect on sales. (*The Petroleum Industry, p. 144.*)

W. H. NICHOLLS:

Agriculture is particularly vulnerable in [an unstable] economy, because (1) it maintains production even in the face of ruinously low prices; . . . ("A Price Policy . . ." *Journal of Farm Economics,* XXVII [1945], 744.)

This list of demonstrations by academic students could be continued indefinitely, but now I must turn briefly to the business community:

Steel:

. . . the demand for steel is very inelastic. (*U. S. Steel Corporation T. N. E. C. Papers,* v. i, p. 169.)

Cement:

I never found that the company who made those reductions in price obtained any benefit from it whatsoever. If they reduced the price they might have gotten one particular contract, . . . but, in the end, they go[t] no more business, . . . (President Brobston of Hercules; *333 U. S. Supreme Court Briefs and Records 683-740,* v. ii, p. *7697-8.*)

Automobiles:

I do not consider that the present price level of automobiles will have any material bearing on the industry over the twelve months' period. Without question, the prices as announced at the shows were rather a shock to the automobile purchasing public, . . . the objection to price will level itself off within a very short time. (A sales manager, *Automotive Industries,* December 4, 1937, *p. 811.*)

49

Indigo:

An increase in price by all suppliers would undoubtedly disabuse the buyers' minds of the impression now general that an indigo price reduction is imminent and to this extent would greatly strengthen present demand. (Mitsui Trading Company, in Hearings on S2303, Senate Committee on Patents, 77th Congress, 2nd Session, *p. 2380.*)

For the most comprehensive and authoritative information, however, one must turn to the experience of men who have controlled large sectors of the economy. Before the war was over, OPA had characterized almost all salable things in the American economy except economists' services in terms such as these:

The increased use of southern pine lumber stemming from the defense program and the accompanying expanded economic activity has caused demand to exceed supply [sic]. As a consequence, inflationary pressure has caused prices to rise greatly in excess of previously existing industry levels. (Price Schedule No. 19, November 24, 1941, *p. 1.*)

As a result of the much increased demand and the temptation to speculation which this has provided, prices of cattle tail hair and winter hog hair have shown sharp increases which are not warranted by any increase in cost of production and which can have little effect in augmenting the supply. (*Price Schedule No. 24*, August 27, 1941, *p. 1.*)

Of course some of these passages could be interpreted as meaning that the demand curve had merely shifted far to the right, and was not necessarily inelastic. But a variety of ancillary considerations oppose this interpretation. The uses of subsidies and differential prices usually rested on inelasticity of supply. The use of allocations, rationing, and priorities rested on inelasticities of demand. Every price rise was "unwarranted"; but the warrant of a price rise is to encourage supply and/or ration demand; hence the OPA economists meant that higher prices would fail to perform these functions. Moreover, when pressed they will concede that price control was successful because it kept down index numbers of prices, i.e., it had no appreciable effects on output.

And finally, let us look to Great Britain where, economic events being centrally planned, all supply and demand functions are known. Here the evidence of ubiquitous inelasticity is silently impressive: in the economic plan (as reported in the *Economic Survey for 1948*) no reference is made to relative prices. For example,

In the United States we are making great efforts to increase our exports, but any really large expansion would require a radical change in the importing habits of that country. (*p. 10*)

That is, lower prices would not increase American dollar purchases. Again, in dealing with excess peak demand for electricity, several devices are alluded to as possible solutions (*pp. 24-6*), but no reference is made to raising rates, which therefore must be ineffective. All in all, this—one may say, deliberate and systematic—disregard of prices is powerful evidence for the law.

I therefore consider the empirical evidence overwhelming. Of course elastic demands have sometimes been alleged, usually without any real evidence. But in at least two cases, evidence of a sort has been proffered:

Cranberry Sauce:

Assuming income per head at the preceding year's level, the market can be expected to absorb every year a 17.5 per cent increase in the quantity of cranberry sauce marketed, without a decline in price. Every per cent increase in quantity *in excess of* *17.5 per cent* over the previous year would *depress* the price by 0.49 per cent below the previous year's level. (C. D. Hyson and F. H. Sanderson, "Monopolistic Discrimination in the Cranberry Industry," *Quarterly Journal of Economics,* LIX (1944-45), 348, 350.)

Domestic Servants:

The price elasticity . . . has an even greater absolute value: —2.3 (G. J. Stigler, *Domestic Servants in the United States, 1900-40, pp. 30, 32.*)

These adverse examples are not necessarily proof of the ineptitude of the investigators: they can be explained very simply as the result of Sampling Fluctuations.

A Priori Demonstration

I shall give two proofs that all demand curves are in-elastic. Each covers most of the economy; the two together surely cover all industries once and most industries twice; but I do not wish to purchase elegance with uncertainty. Thereafter the elasticity of supply will be examined.

First, Marshall's proof:

The third condition [for inelastic demand] is that only a small part of the expenses of production of the commodity should consist of the price of this factor. Since the plasterer's wages are but a small part of the total expenses of building a house, a rise of even 50 per cent in them would add but a very small percentage to the expenses of production of a house and would check demand but little. (*Principles of Economics, p. 385.*)

Now, almost every product is a small part of the expense of some other product: steel accounts for only a tenth of the cost of an automobile; transportation charges are a small part of delivered prices; the cost of a home is a small part of the cost of living. Thus most demand curves are inelastic.[1] It may be noted that Marshall assumed for purposes of this argument that no substitution is possible among the various inputs; who can question his right to do this?

Second, the expectation proof. When prices rise, no one will buy less of commodities, because prices are expected to rise further; and when prices fall, no one buys more, because prices are expected to fall further. The anticipation of purchases when prices rise, and the postponement of purchases when prices fall, serve to confirm and continue the expectations. (Some economists go on to say that the way to decrease quantity demanded—and increase quantity supplied—is to lower prices, but this may be making too much of a good thing.)

No one can question the general validity of this proof, but in this—its usual—form it lacks refinement and rigor. The first price change does not set off the anticipations; clearly it was also anticipated. And a seller anticipates in the case of price reductions, for example, that the first reduction would simply confirm buyers' anticipations and not help sales, so he may make the reduction in two steps to eliminate anticipation of further decreases. But, of course, the buyers can easily anticipate this. So the seller cuts the price exactly the amount they anticipated, just to get it over with, but this they did not anticipate, so business deteriorates. The seller never anticipated this result, so in panic he makes an unanticipated further price change, and at this, business of course comes to a halt. After certain further, obvious steps, which

1. This proof has an august corollary. Since most or all specific costs of production are relatively small, and entrepreneurs do not bother with small costs, therefore they do not bother with costs at all. Hence they do not maximize profits. This corollary has implications for economic theory.

I shall omit for brevity's sake, price eventually settles down. Sales resume, at the old rate, it is to be anticipated.

The careful reader will have noticed that supply has received little attention; this gap will now be filled. The fact is, that inelastic demands imply inelastic supplies; hence it is sufficient to prove the existence of the former. Some economists are so inconsistent as to say demands are inelastic but that marginal cost curves are horizontal; the following proof will show that this is ill-advised.

First, an intuitive proof. If the demand for input A is inelastic, a 10 per cent decrease in its price leads to less than a 10 per cent increase in the quantity taken; and similarly for other inputs. If all input prices decrease 10 per cent, an even smaller increase in the quantity of A that is taken will occur, for substitution incentives disappear; and similarly for other inputs. But a fall of 10 per cent in the price of each input is equivalent to a rise of (about) 11 per cent in the price of product. Therefore an 11 per cent rise in the price of the product leads to less than a 10 per cent increase of each input, and therefore to less than a 10 per cent increase of output, so supply is inelastic. This proof is deficient in that it glosses over the possibility of extreme complementarity of inputs; the deficiency will be removed Mathematically.

Let us define some symbols:

$$x = \text{output,}$$
$$a, b = \text{inputs,}$$
$$p, p_a, p_b = \text{respective prices,}$$
$$x = \phi\,(a, b) = \text{production function.}$$

The conditions for maximum profit are,

$$p\varphi_a = p_a; \qquad p\varphi_b = p_b.$$

Differentiate these equations partially with respect to p_a, and then with respect to p_b; and define the symbols:

$$\Delta = \begin{vmatrix} \varphi_{aa} & \varphi_{ab} \\ \varphi_{ab} & \varphi_{bb} \end{vmatrix},$$

$$\eta_a = \frac{\partial a}{\partial p_a}\frac{p_a}{a},$$

$$\eta_b = \frac{\partial b}{\partial p_b}\frac{p_b}{b},$$

$$\eta_{ab} = \frac{\partial b}{\partial p_a}\frac{p_a}{b}.$$

Then

$$\eta_a = p_a\varphi_{bb}/ap\Delta,$$

$$\eta_b = p_b\varphi_{aa}/bp\Delta,$$

$$\eta_{ab} = -p_a\varphi_{ab}/bp\Delta.$$

Now differentiate the maximum profit equations with respect to p, to obtain,

$$\frac{\partial a}{\partial p} = (p_b\varphi_{ab} - p_a\varphi_{bb})/p^2\Delta,$$

$$\frac{\partial b}{\partial p} = (p_a\varphi_{ab} - p_b\varphi_{aa})/p^2\Delta.$$

Finally, the elasticity of supply is

$$\eta_s = \frac{\partial x}{\partial p}\frac{p}{x} = \frac{p}{x}\left(\varphi_a\frac{\partial a}{\partial p} + \varphi_b\frac{\partial b}{\partial p}\right).$$

If one substitutes around a bit, and defines k_a as ap_a/xp, and similarly for k_b, he will reach this equation:

$$\eta_s = k_a|\eta_a| + k_b|\eta_b| - 2k_b\eta_{ab}.$$

We recall that we have shown that $|\eta_a| < 1$, $|\eta_b| < 1$. The implications are unambiguous:

(1) If $\eta_{ab} > 0$ (inputs are substitutes),

$$\eta_s < 1, \text{ for } k_a|\eta_a| + k_b|\eta_b| < 1.$$

(2) If perchance $\eta_{ab} < 0$, we notice that if $\Delta > 0$, as stability of equilibrium recommends, then

$$k_a\eta_a\eta_b > k_b\eta^2_{ab}.$$

At worst, therefore,

$$\eta_s < (\sqrt{k_a|\eta_a|} + \sqrt{k_b|\eta_b|})^2$$

But the expression on the right can be assumed, with no loss of specificity, to be less than unity.   Q. E. D.

Implications

THE TERMINOLOGICAL implication is that demands and supplies with elasticities of zero should be called inelastic; those with elasticities numerically less than unity, elastic. Elasticity has the same range of variation as the coefficient of correlation, correctly calculated.

The discussion of the economic implications must be reserved for another occasion, on which it will be shown that there is no price system.

This letter to an admired friend proposed a method of raising the technical quality of professional writing. He accepted its feasibility, and I still do, but I was unattracted by the task. I owe apologies to Professor Hansen for choosing his work as an example, especially since some of mine would serve as well!

8

On Scientific Writing

IN THE September 1947 issue of the *American Economic Review,* Hansen states (p. 563):

. . . of the $60 billion gross capital formation in business plant and equipment made in the decade 1931-40, 90 per cent was replacement investment.

His colleague, Harris, writing in the later-appearing August issue of the *Review of Economic Statistics,* states (p. 152):

But let us not forget that for the decade of the thirties, gross investment was but $60 billion and *net* investment was approximately zero.

The comparison suggests at least four comments:

1. The same figure is given for two rather different series; business capital is only part of total capital.
2. The amount of net investment differs.
3. Neither man gives any reference for his figures.
4. The probable source is the Department of Commerce, which has no series with these titles. The most plausible series do not approximate Hansen's $60 billion nor his 90 per cent.

This almost studied carelessness in the use of facts is very common in economic literature. It is not necessary, or even proper, for me to emphasize to a perfectionist like you the objections to this sort of work. There may be deception. If these errors are widespread and increasing, we may have to give up division of labor. In any event, such errors are more than a symptom of general sloppiness of thought and research procedures—they are an integral part of that sloppiness. Nor do I need to argue the desirability of improving the quality of economic research and writing.

I believe that real improvements could be obtained by checking a large range of economic literature and publishing the results of the checking. Let me spell out this proposal:

The Types of Error

ECONOMISTS POSSESS their full share of the common ability to invent and commit errors: copying a number wrong, forgetting to tell what number it is or where they go it, making arithmetical mistakes, relying upon fickle memory, etc. They can reason fallaciously, with or without mathematics. They can misread completely the state of affairs, or reverse the direction of causation. Perhaps their most common error is to believe other economists.

It is impossible to check thoroughly the quality of economic literature, even on a narrow front. Even the most competent economist will be biased in what he checks: he will accept as true the statements or bits of reasoning that he believes and he will examine with critical care the views that are novel or contradictory to those he has been holding. Moreover, there is no ultimate test of validity: even the history of mathematics is studded with universally accepted errors.

Checks of the quality of economic literature should be relatively free of ambiguity as to both [1] what is to be checked, and [2] whether it is correct or erroneous. Two types of material seem capable of fairly large-scale and objective measurement of accuracy:

1. Statements of empirical fact.
2. Quotations from other writers.

Of course one must make concessions to the more or less legitimate desire of an economist to be read. There is no point in checking, or trying to check, [1] sweeping generalizations (capitalism is dying); [2] widely accepted beliefs (a depression started in 1929); [3] the completeness of references to well known sources or series (the cost of living index need not be referred to as compiled by the Bureau of Labor Statistics, referring to clerical and manual workers in 5x large American cities, etc.). Nor would I attempt to check paraphrases of the writings of other people, except where specific numbers are involved, since arguable points arise immediately.

The checking of fairly specific statements seems to me eminently useful for two reasons. First, it is not probable that a man who is careless in small matters is careful in large ones; quite the contrary, a man who cannot even copy a sentence of Keynes's correctly is not likely to be a reliable reporter of complicated or badly expressed ideas. Second, it is precisely in these narrower matters that the reader is most at the writer's mercy: a reputable economist, writing in a reputable journal, acquires an aura of reliability, and after all, we cannot check many things and still do our own work.

The Measurement of Errors

I PROPOSE that all of the leading American economic journals for some recent year be used as the bases of the tests. This insures variety of authorship and subject, and permits no invidious selection. A group of graduate students could subject each empirical statement and quotation to verification, given suitable training and supervision. I have not explored the problem sufficiently to have very definite ideas on the nature of the tests, but two examples suggest their general nature.

Empirical statements. Hansen, in the article referred to, makes 16 distinct statements of a specific nature about prices and capital formation. Among the relevant tests are:

1. Frequency and accuracy of source. He gives no sources.
2. Adequacy of description. One series—retail food prices—is adequately described; "prices" refers to wholesale prices; "finished goods prices" is a title abandoned 5 to 10 years ago for "manufactured goods prices"; and his capital formation series is ambiguous.
3. Frequency of error. 8 of his 16 statements are wrong.

Possibly something could also be done on the magnitude of error. In Hansen's article, for example, 3 of the 8 errors exceeded 5 per cent of the correct figure.

Quotations. Here I take Marshall's *Principles* because of its great importance, despite the fact that it was written in an age of more informal scholarship. Of 107 quotations of English sources which were traced, only 50 were correct (or deviated only in punctuation or detail). Of the 57 incorrect quotations, two (both from Smith!) departed in a significant degree from the original. Only 72 of the 107 citations of sources could be considered remotely adequate.

In articles based on calculations, it would be possible to assess the adequacy of the descriptions, and the accuracy of the results. But a complete verification of a year's work would be a very large task indeed, and perhaps some sampling would be called for.

The Benefits of the Study

THE BENEFITS of such a study, duly publicized, appear to me to be several and substantial:

1. Economists will be taught a decent caution as readers; we are all too prone to accept unquestioningly the printed word or number.

2. There should be an immediate improvement in the low editorial standards of most of our journals; every editor would edit with more care and demand more adequate references.

3. The tests will remind economists that footnotes are not an occasional token of respect for an obsolete and purposeless tradition. It will come as a shock to many, I am sure, even to realize that references can be checked.

4. The study may lead to the improvement in the quality of training of graduate students. Most teachers are unaware of the problem of quality, so naturally their students are too. Indeed, the checking of references may become a standard pastime of malicious

graduate students—which would be more useful to the students and the profession than the activities of malicious graduate students as I partook in them.

I should be very interested in your opinion of the feasibility and desirability of such a project.

This ancient piece is included only because careless students may be thus enticed to buy this volume.

9

How to Pass Examinations in Economics

STUDENTS always display a powerful, not to say unhealthy, interest in how to answer questions in examinations on economics. They can do fairly well with the essay, or subjective, questions, but they do not seem at home with the true-false, or objective, questions. And yet these latter questions are very easy, as I shall show. I shall develop the proper techniques by using questions from *Students Manual to Accompany the Elements of Economics* by Lorie Tarshis by Lorie Tarshis and Phillip Cartwright.[1] Sooner or later the able students will discover that the appendix to the manual gives the answers to the true-false questions (which are called comprehension tests), so it will save time if I reproduce the answers with the questions.

---

1. That is, the book is by Tarshis and the manual is by Tarshis and Cartwright. Of course, the manual is a book too.

It is very important that the student gain self-confidence, so I shall begin with a simple example:

9. Taxes constitute a part of fixed costs. $\underline{F^2}$

The indicated answer of F is of course T. It is important to note that this answer has a very general validity, E.G.,

9A. Taxes do not constitute a part of fixed costs. $\underline{F}$

9B. Taxes constitute a part of variable costs. $\underline{F}$

9C. Taxes do not constitute a part of variable costs. $\underline{F}$

Every cost, it must be remembered, is fixed or variable, and not both simultaneously. A tax is a cost. But some taxes vary with output and some don't, and the statement refers to taxes in the plural. This means that perhaps both fixed and variable taxes are being referred to. Hence the statement is partly right, part of the time, and therefore false.

Lesson 1: A statement that can be false, is false.

Since we are on the subject of taxes, let us tackle the next question, which is rather more difficult:

10. A tax on corporation profits is a variable cost. $\underline{F}$

The student could easily fall into a trap of his own construction here. He might reason: the corporation tax varies with the corporation's profits, and the profits vary with output, so the corporation tax varies with output.

Lesson 2: A tax on corporation profits is not a variable cost.

Now that self-confidence has been gained, it is necessary to acquire humility:

2. P. 17. F means fantastic.

6. If firms do not seek to maximize profits, their output will not be that at which the marginal cost and revenue are equal.   T[3]

The lads who think they are clever will argue: if the firm doesn't care about profits, might it not accidentally operate at this output? And by Lesson 1, that would make the statement false. But let's see where such superficial cleverness leads: such a student will feel impelled to answer the following question as follows:

6A. If firms seek not to maximize profits, their output will not be that at which the marginal cost and revenue are equal. T (Really F)

For one thing, marginal cost equals marginal revenue also at minimum profits. For another thing, a firm can make a mistake, can't it? To return to the original question, everything is a matter of probability. There are many possible outputs, and probably only one maximizes profits. Besides, profits usually aren't maximized when marginal cost equals (total) revenue.

Lesson 3: A statement that can be true, is true.

In preparing for an examination in economics, it is desirable to study the economy for years and thus acquire a feel for the facts. See how realistic insight helps on this one:

7. If a tax of 3¢ per unit is imposed on the product of a perfectly competitive industry, the price will rise by exactly 3¢.   F[4]

This statement is false for three reasons: there are no perfectly competitive industries; if there were, they would not be constant cost industries; and if they were, they wouldn't raise the price of a locomotive by just 3 cents.

3. P. 44. T means theoretically.   4. P. 62.

Lesson 4: Know your economy.

Even a good student will sometimes overlook a section
of the economy or the textbook. Even so, formal logic may
come to his rescue:

10. Although theoretically the control of a corporation
is vested in all of its owners, in actual fact the control of most corporations rests with their elected
directors.   T[5]

Remember page 58: "Theory and practice should not con-
tradict one another." So if in theory the owners control the
corporation, then in fact they do; if in fact the directors control the corporations, then in theory they do. Hence owners
and directors are identical. Once we know this, the answer
follows directly.

Lesson 5: Know your logic.

I now turn to Keynesian economics, one of the more
difficult branches of economic theory. I begin with a troublesome question:

1. If prices are inflexible, an increase in the wage rates
paid by one firm will not lead it to dismiss employees.   T[6]

The key to this question is that wages rise only for one firm.
Hence this firm hires kinds of labor that no other firm hires
(unless it is being discriminated against, cruelly). If it did
fire any workers, where could they go? The entrepreneur is
a decent chap.

5. P. 11. Tarshis, or Tarshis and Cartwright, are probably the only
economists who have studied the distribution of control in the hundreds
of thousands of corporations. _____?

6. P. 124.

Lesson 6:   Not every entrepreneur is greedy.

Of course some Keynesian economics is very simple. For example,

1. If investment rises from 40 to 45 and then remains steady at 45, the national income will rise very rapidly and then rise at a slower rate.   F⁷

This is very easy, and indeed I put it in just as a breather before the next question. Since it required 87 years and 3 months for investment to rise from 40 just to 41, why should the national income rise very rapidly?

Lesson 7:   Read and write carefully.

Now I come to a question that has the full flavor of the Keynesian theory:

7. Neglecting the acceleration effects, public investment directed to useless projects enriches the country.   T⁸

Since I have not read this chapter of Tarshis' book, I do not know his precise explanation. No doubt it is very similar to mine: Governments are so foolish that they are more likely to do good when they don't try than when they do. This reminds me that an economist, named Harrod, recently wrote a pamphlet in which he argued that a country (named England) was getting impoverished because there was too much useful public investment. Oddly enough, Harrod (who is writing the official life of Keynes) claims Keynes would agree with him!

7. P. 98.   8. P. 115. It also enriches the city.

Lesson 8: Not everybody understands Keynesian economics.

Finally, I want to emphasize how important it is for the student to keep his wits about him:

4. Farmers suffer as much in depression as do wage-earners.   T (Really F[9])

The wrong answer was given in the appendix, I am sure, to see if the student had been lulled into a state of uncritical receptiveness. It stands to reason that farmers do not suffer as much as do wage-earners. For one thing, there aren't as many farmers. For another thing, it is not very probable that farmers suffer *exactly* as much as wage-earners.

Lesson 9: Nobody knows the suffering farmers[10] do.

9. P. 88.   10. And students.

Vulgar luxury has always been condemned by men of high taste and income. Economists have lent some support to their displeasure, and I add my mite.

10

The Alarming Cost of Model Changes: A Case Study

FRANKLIN FISHER, Zvi Griliches, and Carl Kaysen have shown, in an article which will command wide and respectful attention, that if consumers had been content with the 1949 automobile, they would be saving over $700 per car by 1961.[1] They properly have left open the question whether improvements such as greater speeds and automatic transmissions were worth the cost, but after all, the 1949 cars ran, and kept out the rain.[2] Perhaps the $5 billion a year of extra costs had better alternative uses—higher tuition fees, more adequate farm subsidies, a violin in every home.

Their choice of the automobile industry was arbitrary,

1. "The Costs of Automobile Model Changes Since 1949," *Journal of Political Economy*, October, 1962.
2. My 1950 Dodge was considerably more efficient in the latter role than in the former, however.

but reasonable; there has been much comment on over-elaborate automobiles; it is a large industry; and annual model changes are a prominent feature of its behavior. Of course, every sector—even public schools and health—displays a mixture of frivolous and genuine improvements, and eventually, let us hope, estimates of the costs of product changes will be available for all. I propose here to estimate the costs for an industry in which model changes have reached an almost unbelievable pitch.

The industry is publishing, and I was led to it by the comparison of editions of the same work. It is essentially correct that a man never changes, and seldom improves on, his views: certainly this is true of Ricardo (3 editions), Mill (7 editions), Marshall (8 editions), Böhm-Bawerk (3 editions), Walras (5 editions), Pigou (4 editions), Roscher (27 editions), etc. I suspect that the revision every five years of our textbooks reflects market considerations more than it expresses the march of scientific progress. The costs of this sort of minor amendment are not negligible—unlike the automobile, the older editions lose their usefulness.

But the phenomenon of change goes much deeper. Each year we publish about 11,000 books in the United States. Not *one* is in the list of 100 greatest books. Why must we have the *Rise and Fall of the Third Reich,* when the *Rise and Fall of the Dutch Republic* is a better book, and in the public domain? Is the *Tropic of Cancer* better (worse) than the works of the Marquis de Sade? What, precisely, are the respects in which Tennessee Williams surpasses Shakespeare? Samuelson (5 editions), Bach (3 editions), Harriss (4 editions) and others write our textbooks; is it abundantly clear that they are better books than the *Wealth of Nations*?

The economist cannot answer these questions. The answers rest on value judgments, which are not scientific, and the economist is a scientist. All the economist can do is report the facts. As Fisher, Griliches, and Kaysen say, we cannot tell a drunkard to stop drinking, but we can audit the bar bill. Or, to choose a metaphor without normative overtones, we cannot tell a nation to stop turning beautiful trees into waste paper, but we can weigh the ashes.

So let us assume that no new books were printed after 1900. This date is less arbitrary than 1949, I think, and in any event it yields bigger numbers. Some books of this earlier period would probably sell in only small quantities (I have in mind an item such as J. S. Mill's *An Examination of Sir William Hamilton's Philosophy, and of the Principal Philosophical Questions Discussed in His Writings* or Sinclair's 21 volume survey of Scotland in 1791-99), although without the diversion of the new models their markets would strengthen. Some books might even disappear (I have in mind such an item as Heinrich's *Phlogiston ist die Wahrheit*). But there would be an ample selection of reading matter: the books of 1900 and before could not run or keep out the rain, but they could furnish the minds of Newton, Gauss, Beethoven, and Goethe, of Jefferson and Lincoln and Dred Scott.

The stream of savings would be immense, and it would be fed by a thousand hidden springs. Let me just cite four important components:

1. All books would be royalty free, with savings of perhaps 10 per cent on retail prices. The authors would usually have alternative products.

2. The plates of a typical book now print about 3,000 copies. This could be raised to at least 200,000 with a reduction of 98.5 per cent in composition costs. Easily another 30 per cent reduction in price. (This item alone exceeds the savings in the automobile study, as a percent of price.)

3. Advertising of books would fall, perhaps by 98 per cent. This would cut prices another 5 or 10 per cent.

71

4. In happy analogy to Fisher, Griliches, and Kaysen, books would get more mileage. Once a family outside Wisconsin grew up, its sturdily bound McGuffy Readers could be passed on to a second generation, and possibly a third. This would reduce costs by a factor of 2.5, making the aggregate saving perhaps 85 per cent of present costs.

I shall not pause to estimate indirect savings: houses could be smaller; people would not have to change the prescription of their glasses so often; teachers would not have to think up new examination questions; etc.

When we turn to newspapers, the savings would be even greater. There is nothing new under the sun, so it would be sufficient to print a dozen volumes of news once and for all: crimes, wars, women, colonies, frontier life, emancipation, and the Irish Question, for example. In addition to a saving of say 98 per cent on newspapers, there would be a substantial reduction in efforts by people to get into the news.

These savings are to be calculated in the billions of dollars, and the billions of hours of reader time. There would be some delay in the dissemination of new knowledge, few changes are without costs. I would beg the reader, however, to keep two facts in mind: most new knowledge is false; and the news got around in Athens.

The report of the task force created by the American Economic Association to improve the teaching of economics in the high school will become an important influence on our school system. These critical remarks were prepared for a symposium on the report.

11

Elementary Economic Education

THE TASK FORCE appointed by the American Economic Association and financed by the Committee for Economic Development has reported on the problem of instruction in economics in the high school. The task force contained five highly esteemed economists: G. L. Bach (chairman), Lester Chandler, R. A. Gordon, Ben Lewis, and Paul Samuelson; as well as two specialists in secondary education, Arno Bellack and M. L. Frankel. Although the American Economic Association explicitly does not endorse the report, it chose the economists and hence certified to their competence and distinction. No other body concerned with economic education has had such professional status, nor is an equally authoritative body likely to appear in this decade. The report will therefore command an audience of unusual size and deference among high school and college teachers.

This unusual status is, I believe, unfortunate. The economists composing the task force are leaders in American economics, of unquestionable competence and integrity. But they do not monopolize these virtues, and their special mode of selection serves to give their views an eminence which is incompatible with the doctrine of free competition (= free discussion) in educational and scientific work. The views of the task force will receive a respectful but critical reading by professional economists; they will not receive anything like so critical a scrutiny by the people in charge of elementary economic education. If—to use an unbelievably remote possibility—I or some other professional reviewer convicted them of error, the important audience would never learn of it.

To this lament on professional sponsorship there is a clear and weighty response. If there is not an authoritative professional influence on high school instruction in economics, what other sources of influence will prevail? The answer is: a strange medley of [1] teachers and school administrators long on pedagogy and short on economics, [2] special interest groups who flood our schools with variously slanted materials, and [3] a rearguard of textbook salesmen and opinionated local school board members. And has not this strange and not always open competition led to a generally unsatisfactory neglect and/or treatment of economics in the high school?

I have no counterresponse to offer. I even believe that the task force's schemes are better by almost every economist's values than those which now on average prevail. It is for each person to decide whether benevolent monopoly is ever justifiable in the realm of education. My own preference is clear: of all monopolies, that of opinions is worst.

74

Let us abandon this question, and look at two other problems which the report raises. The first concerns policy slant, the second concerns pedagogical feasibility.

Readers will know that the report has already been criticized as absurdly neutral toward communism and filled with soft welfare state views—by the conservative press. They can conjecture—as I do, since I missed *The Daily Worker* that day—that the other extreme thinks the task force sold out to Wall Street.

I do not propose to discuss the political slant of the report in any detail. It is fair to say that the committee which wrote the report does not include a representative of the extreme 10 per cent of economists at each end of the distribution of economists—neither fervent free market disciples nor extreme interventionists were represented. Since the committee consisted of men who are representative of the central range of professional opinion, one can hardly call its position unrepresentative.

This does not mean that the report is in any sense "impartial"—indeed I do not know anyone who is impartial or, if he is, how we can know it. I strongly disagree, for example, with the implicit verdict of the task force (and presumably of the profession) that although the problems posed by monopoly deserve extensive discussion (*pp. 33-36*), no comparable issues are raised by public regulation (*p. 36*). But obviously neither a Professor Bach nor I can presently persuade the other that he is wrong or—being honest men—we would have resolved our differences earlier. The only legitimate complaint—and I promise not to recur to this point—is that some (representative) views have been given a preferential status among noneconomists.

Let us turn finally to what the task force believes should be in the high school course in economics: "The minimal understanding needed for effective citizenship in the modern

75

American economy" (*p. 22*). Here full quotation is essential, but the reader will find it sufficient to sample the list. Only their explicit demands for inclusion of topics are listed, although this rule omits subjects which the task force believes to be very important (E.G., *p. 52*), but probably for reasons of elegant variation chose not to introduce with a "Students should know. . . ."

It is important that students understand the central role which markets and prices play in this process [of selecting the goods to produce and the way in which to produce them]. (*p. 28*)

Students should have a general picture of the national stock of such resources, and of the way in which this stock has grown over the years. (*p. 28*)

Students should see that the high American standard of living depends on a combination of all these factors [governing productivity]. . . . (*p. 29*)

. . . the student should understand the relationships between *saving, investment,* and *capital formation.* (*p. 29*)

Students should also understand, in broad terms, the *principle of diminishing returns.* (*p. 30*)

It is important for students to see that there are three main types of participants in economic activity. (*p. 30*)

Individual freedom of choice is central to the "private enterprise way." It is essential that students understand both what this freedom does and does not mean, and also how a private enterprise economy manages to get its business done when individuals are free to make their own economic decisions. (*p. 31*)

To comprehend the working of markets, the student must understand the main determinants of demand and supply. (*p. 32*)

Students should know something of the intent and nature of laws designed to enforce competition, and should understand something of the process by which such legislation is enforced through the courts and federal administrative agencies. (*pp. 34-35*)

Students should be familiar with these trends [in competition] in a general way and, particularly in their history courses, should have the opportunity to look briefly at the development of trusts, holding companies, and other forms of mergers over the past century. (*p. 35*)

In connection with corporations, it is desirable for students to have a grasp of a *simple* balance sheet and income statement, reflecting only the four or five major categories in each. (*p. 36*)

Students should also understand the important function performed by securities exchanges, which permit investors to buy and sell readily securities which have already been issued. (*p. 36*)

It is important for students to understand that, even in a basically free enterprise economy, governments play a significant role in setting priorities and using resources—that is, in deciding what to produce and how to produce it. (p. 37)

Students should have some impression of the order of magnitude of government spending, which now accounts for over a quarter of the national income. (*p. 38*)

Students should have a general impression of the major taxes currently used. (*p. 39*)

. . . it is important that the student be introduced to the study of international economic relations. (p. 39)

Students should be given a brief introduction to the concept of the international balance of payments. (p. 40)

One point that should be emphasized with students is the difference between the *balance of trade* and the *balance of payments*. (*p. 41*)

Students need to be introduced to the fact that many of our greatest economic problems center around how to obtain stable economic growth, avoiding the excesses of the inflationary booms and depressions. (p. 43)

Students should be familiar with the concept [of gross national product], although technical details should be avoided. (*p. 44*)

Students need to be impressed with the fact that this element of *dynamic interdependence* is a highly important feature of all money-using, private-enterprise economies. (*p. 46*)

Students should see that the burden imposed upon the taxpayer by a growing public debt depends largely on how rapidly the national income is rising. (*p. 47*)

Although students should be introduced to money and banking, it is too much to hope that they can master all of the intricacies about them which are found in college textbooks. (*p. 48*)

Every informed person should understand how new deposits are created when banks make loans or buy securities, and how deposits are correspondingly reduced when bank loans are repaid or the banks sell securities which they have been holding. (*p. 49*)

The Federal Reserve can control the reserves of the commercial banks which the latter must keep as backing for the public's deposits. Students need understand in only a very general way how this can be done, by raising or lowering commercial bank reserve requirements and through "open market operations." (*p. 50*)

Students need to understand that we should not expect monetary management to do things that it cannot do, and that we should not damn it for sins of which it is innocent. (*p. 50*)

But students should be able to see that if a country loses gold, it is likely (or may even be forced) to tighten credit conditions. (*p. 51*)

It is important for students to understand the vast difference between conditions here and in the underdeveloped economies, and to appreciate some of the problems such economies face. (*p. 53*)

Students should understand how money incomes arise out of the sale of productive services by individuals to businesses and governments. Equally important, they should understand that these money incomes provide the means of obtaining "real income"— that is, the goods and services that people buy with their money incomes. (*p. 55*)

Students should know in broad outline of the distribution of personal incomes in the United States, including their own place in the income structure. (*p. 56*)

Students should understand that high American wages rest fundamentally on the high productivity of American labor. (p. 57)

Every person should understand something of the role of unions in labor-management relations. (p. 58)

The "farm problem" should be understood broadly by students. (p. 59)

Students should be generally familiar with these various arrangements that directly affect their personal economic security. They should also be able to reason objectively about the economic effects, and hence the desirability from different points of view, of these different types of security measures. (p. 60)

Every informed American should have a general impression of how other types of economic systems operate, especially communism. (p. 61)

In addition to being able to compare private enterprise and communism, the student should also be sensitively aware of the fact that various democratic societies—the United Kingdom, the Scandinavian countries, and India, for example—have chosen to adopt socialism in varying degrees. (p. 63)

AMEN!

This list of things a high school student should know is, of course, a representative table of contents of a textbook on elementary economics at the college level. Since high school seniors are slightly less mature and substantially less selected than college freshmen, and since high school economics teachers are appreciably less well trained in economics than the instructors in college courses, I take it as rigorously implied that if our present college courses are failing to teach students economics, the proposed high school course will fail by a greater margin.

This is in fact my thesis: the watered-down encyclopedia which constitutes the present course in beginning college economics does not teach the student how to think on economic questions. The brief exposure to each of a vast array of techniques and problems leaves with the student no basic economic logic with which to analyze the economic questions he will face as a citizen. The student will memorize a few facts, diagrams, and policy recommendations, and ten years later will be as untutored in economics as the day he entered the class.

This is bold pronouncement, and gains no authority by coming from a teacher who is many years away from his last course in elementary economics. The thesis will be rejected more completely, I believe, by the teachers of elementary economics than by the textbook writers: it is instructive that the successful textbooks keep *adding* subject matter to their successive editions in response to market demands.

But the thesis that our present college courses (and *a fortiori* the proposed high school course) fail to impart any permanently useful economic training runs against faith, not evidence. I propose the following test:

Select an adequate sample of seniors (I would prefer men five years out of college), equally divided between those who have never had a course in economics and those who have had a conventional one-year course. Give them an examination on current economic problems—*not* on textbook questions. I predict they will not differ in their performance.

I shall illustrate below the kind of question that should be asked in this test.

An introductory-terminal course in economics makes its greatest contribution to the education of students if it concentrates upon a few subjects, which are developed in sufficient detail and applied to a sufficient variety of actual economic problems to cause the student to absorb the basic logic of the approach. The few subjects should be chosen with a view to their importance (which includes the frequency with which they are encountered) and to what present-day economics has to contribute to their understanding. Both criteria, I believe, argue for an immense concentration on price theory—the allocation of resources and the pricing of goods and services.

It seems almost beyond dispute that the citizen is called upon overwhelmingly, indeed almost exclusively, to pass on policies governing the allocation of resources and the formation of prices. I consider this proposition to be self-evident in the area of state and local governmental policies; and it is hardly less true of national economic problems. I made a more or less complete count of the bills which were passed by the first session of the 81st Congress (1959) to get the following tabulation of bills with a strong or exclusively economic interest:

1. Disposal of national resources and Indian lands
    At least 71, of which general bills numbered   5
2. Regulation of economic activity
    Agriculture   13
    Merchant Marine   7
    Housing   6
    Highways   6
    Labor   7
    Other: banking, air pollution, imports, etc.   22
3. Taxation (individual taxes)   9
4. Tax exemption   5
5. General appropriation acts   16
6. Selective expenditures
    Salaries   12
    Veterans   11
    Other   29
7. Monetary policy   3

To the extent that the economist has anything to say in these areas, he uses price theory 99 times for every instance in which income and employment theory has any relevance.

81

Questions directed primarily to maintaining employment are posed so infrequently, and are even then (as in the appropriation acts) so completely dominated by allocative questions that for practical purposes they are an infrequent and minor problem for the citizen.

If the elementary course were to recognize the civic pre-eminence of traditional value and distribution theory, it would spend much less time on other parts of economics. And if it recognized the immense variety of allocation problems, and the impossibility of giving a mastery of detailed techniques to the one-year student, it would concentrate on the essential logic of competition and monopoly, of consumer choice, and of the theory of wages. The student would be taught, not elasticities or envelopes or oligopolistic models, but the central issues of analysis and fact in questions such as:[1]

HR. 236

To prohibit discrimination because of age in the hiring and employment of persons by government contractors.

HR. 1251

To authorize a five-year program of grants and scholarships for collegiate education in the field of nursing.

HR. 2895

To grant a pension of $100 a month to all honorably discharged veterans of World War I who are over 62 years of age.

HR. 5983

To enable producers to provide a supply of turkeys adequate to meet the needs of consumers, to maintain orderly marketing con-

1. The list is from unsuccessful bills of the first session, 81st Congress, but the headlines of the newspapers will do as well.

ditions, and to promote and expand the consumption of turkeys and turkey products.

HR. 7714

To define, regulate, and license television service contractors.

HR. 9038

To amend the Tariff Act of 1930 to provide for the establishment of country-by-country quotas for the importation of shrimps and shrimp products.

S. 215

To supplement the antitrust laws of the United States by requiring that corporations, in industries so heavily concentrated that monopoly or the threat of monopoly is present, file advance notice and make public justification before effectuating price increases.

I proposed above a test of whether our present elementary courses had any lasting value. The questions that ought to be used in such a test are precisely the current questions of policy. Give the student a summary page or two of the arguments and evidence presented in the discussion (in Congress and the public press) of HR. 5983 (orderly turkeys) and let him explain benefits and costs of the scheme—with the grading based, of course, on the coherence of his argument and relevance of his evidence, not on the conclusions reached.[2]

Let us hope that the test would reveal that our present elementary courses do not have a zero, or negative, value. The test would still leave open the question: Would intense concentration on the basic logic of price theory, applied to

2. Such questions can be preceded by simpler ones such as that which Senator Symington recently flunked: If stockpiles of materials

two score of real problems, give a vastly better and more lasting training than the current encyclopedic texts? Surely, the
answer is yes.

---

owned by the government are given directly to defense contractors
rather than sold in the market, will we not be able to dispose of them
without depressing their prices?

The present piece was written to persuade young intellectuals that we should re-examine the traditional hostility toward private enterprise. I suppose I should not be surprised that it has been more successful in reaffirming businessmen in their faith. This is not an undesirable effect, but a lecturer denouncing cannibalism naturally must view the applause of vegetarians as equivocal evidence of his eloquence.

12

The Intellectual and the Market Place

THE intellectual has never felt kindly toward the market place: to him it has always been a place of vulgar men and of base motives. Whether this intellectual was an ancient Greek philosopher, who viewed economic life as an unpleasant necessity wihch should never be allowed to become obtrusive or dominant, or whether this intellectual is a modern man, who focusses his scorn on gadgets and Madison Avenue, the basic similarity of view has been pronounced.

Now you and I are intellectuals, as this word is used. I am one automatically because I am a professor, and buy more books than golf clubs. You are intellectuals because you are drawn from the most intelligent tenth of the population, most of you will go on to graduate school, and you would rather be a United States Senator or a Nobel Laureate than the head of the Great Atlantic and Pacific Tea Company. The question I wish to pose to us is not whether we should love the market place—even a professor of economics of outrageously conservative tendencies cannot bring himself to say that the chants of five auctioneers rival a Mozart quintet. The questions are rather: what don't we like about the market place; and, are we sure that our attitudes are socially useful?

Let us begin by noticing that from certain important viewpoints one would have expected the intellectuals to be very kindly disposed toward that system of private enterprise which I call the market place.

First, if I may introduce a practical consideration, intellectuals by and large have elevated tastes—they like to eat, dress, and live well, and especially to travel. Walton Hamilton once said that our customary salutation, "Good Day," was a vestige of an agricultural society where people were asking for good weather, and he expected city dwellers eventually to greet each other with the phrase, "Low Prices." If Hamilton's theory is correct, the intellectuals will come to the salutation, "Fair Fulbright."

Since intellectuals are not inexpensive, until the rise of the modern enterprise system, no society could afford many intellectuals. As a wild guess, the full-time intellectuals numbered 200 in Athens in the extraordinary age of Pericles, or about one for every 1500 of population and at most times in later history the intellectuals fell far, far short of this proportion. Today there are at least 1,000,000 in the United States, taking only a fraction of those who live by pen and tongue into account, or one for each 200 of population. At least four out of every five of us owe our pleasant lives to the great achievements of the market place. We professors are much more beholden to Henry Ford than to the foundation which bears his name and spreads his assets.

86

Not only have the productive achievements of the market place supported a much enlarged intellectual class, but also the leaders of the market place have personally been strong supporters of the intellectuals, and in particular those in the academic world. If one asks where, in the western university world, the freedom of inquiry of professors has been most staunchly defended and energetically promoted, my answer is this: Not in the politically controlled universities, whether in the United States or Germany—legislatures are not over-populated with tolerant men indifferent to popularity. Not in the self-perpetuating faculties, such as Oxford and Cambridge from 1700 to 1850—even intellectuals can become convinced that they have acquired ultimate truth, and that it can be preserved indefinitely by airing it before students once a year. No, inquiry has been most free in the college whose trustees are a group of top quality leaders of the market place, men who, our experience shows, are remarkably tolerant of almost everything except a mediocre and complacent faculty. Economics provides many examples: if a professor wishes to denounce aspects of big business, as I have, he will be wise to locate in a school whose trustees are big businessmen, and I have.

But debts are seldom the basis for friendship, and there is a much more powerful reason the intellectual might be sympathetic to the market place: the organizing principles of both areas are the same.

An enterprise system is a system of voluntary contract. Neither fraud nor coercion is within the ethics of the market system. Indeed there is no possibility of coercion in a pure enterprise system because the competition of rivals provides alternatives to every buyer or seller. All real economic systems contain some monopoly, and hence some coercive power for particular individuals, but the amount and the extent of such monopoly power are usually much exaggerated, and in any case monopoly is not an integral part of the logic of the system.

The intellectual world, and I speak chiefly but not exclusively of scholarship, is also a voluntary system. Its central credo is that opinions are to be formed from free discussion on the basis of full disclosure of evidence. Fraud and coercion are equally repugnant to the scholar. The freedom of thought is preserved by the open competition of scholars and ideas. Authority, the equivalent of monopoly power, is the great enemy of freedom of inquiry. Competition in scholarship is in some ways more violent than in business: the law sets limits on the disparagement of a rival's product, unless it is done in a book review in a learned journal.

Just as real markets have some fraud and monopoly, which impair the claims for the market place, so the intellectual world has its instances of coercion and deception, with the coercion exercised by claques and fashion. But again these deviants are outside the logic of the system.

Both areas, moreover, are democratic. The intellectual believes that every able and willing young person should get a good education whatever his race or financial background. The market believes every able and willing person should be permitted to enter an industry or occupation, whatever his race or educational background. There is food for thought in the fact that racial discrimination has diminished earlier, faster, and more quietly in the market place than in political life.

The analogies could be pursued much farther, although not without danger of alienating all professors and most businessmen. I shall therefore merely mention, in passing, that both fields pay a fair amount of attention to packaging and advertising, and both fields place an absurdly high value on originality. There are also many minor differences, such as that the intellectual has no desire to know the market place, whereas the business man wishes, or at least believes he wishes, to know the world of the intellectual. The basic fact is that the intellectual believes in the free market in ideas and, what is not quite the same thing, in words.

Yet whatever the latent sympathies of the intellectual for the market place, the hostilities are overt. The contempt for the "profit motive" which directs economic activity is widespread, and the suspicion of the behavior to which it leads is deep-seated. The charge that American society is materialistic has been recited more often than the Declaration of Independence, and has been translated into more foreign languages.

In one basic respect I believe that the criticism by the intellectuals is misplaced, and at times even hypocritical. The American economy produces many goods that are vulgar, silly, or meretricious, as judged by standards which I share with many intellectuals. It seems only proper to cite a few examples, if only to show how selective these standards are. I shall not propose the currently most popular item, the large and powerful automobile, because I have observed that mostly intellectuals of short stature criticize our cars. But other examples are at hand. I am dissatisfied with the tastes of the nine-tenths of the population which believe that non-fictional books are to be read only by young people working for their B.A. I am dissatisfied with a population whose love for interesting music is so narrow that every symphony orchestra requires subsidies. I consider it shocking that more Americans have read *The Affluent Society* than *The Wealth of Nations*.

At the risk of appearing reasonable, I wish to qualify this complaint by observing that the tastes of the American public are more elevated than those of any other large society in history. Most societies have been judged by their cultural aristocracies—indeed in earlier periods the vast majority of the population was not even considered to be a part of the culture of the society for this vast majority was illiterate, tradition-bound, with most people living brutishly in peasant huts. Our society's tastes are judged by those of the vast majority of the population, and this majority is generous, uncomplacent, and hard-working, with unprecedentedly large numbers engaged in further self-education, or eagerly patronizing the arts. Our market-supported legitimate theatre, which is surely the best in the world, is a suggestive measure of popular tastes.

These qualifications are not intended to withdraw the charge that the public's tastes should be better, and for that matter, that the intellectual's tastes should be better. It is in fact a basic function of the intellectual to define the standards of good taste more clearly, and to persuade people to approach them more closely. It is proper to denounce vulgarity of taste, and to denounce it more strongly the more popular it is. It is permissible to reject certain desires completely—as we do when by compulsory education laws we reject the desire for illiteracy—although there is a strong presumption against the use of force in the area of tastes.

When I say that the complaints of deficiencies in tastes are misplaced when they are directed to the market place, I mean just that. The market place responds to the tastes of consumers with the goods and services that are salable, whether the tastes are elevated or depraved. It is unfair to criticize the market place for fulfilling these desires, when clearly the defects lie in the popular tastes themselves. I consider it a cowardly concession to a false extension of the idea of democracy to make *sub rosa* attacks on public tastes by denouncing the people who serve them. It is like blaming the waiters in restaurants for obesity.

To escape this response, the more sophisticated intellectuals have argued that people are told what to want by the market place—that advertising skillfully depraves and distorts popular desires. There is no doubt an element of truth in this response, but it is an element of trifling size. The advertising industry has no sovereign power to bend men's will—we are not children who blindly follow the last announcer's instructions to rush to the store for soap. Moreover, advertising itself is a completely neutral instrument, and lends itself to the dissemination of highly contradictory desires. While the automobile industry tells us not to drink while driving, the bourbon industry tells us not to drive while drinking. The symphony orchestra advertises, and gets much free publicity, in its rivalry with the dance band. Our colleges use every form of advertising, and indeed the typical university catalogue would never stop Diogenes in his search for an honest man.

So I believe the intellectuals would gain in candor and in grace if they preached directly to the public instead of using advertising as a whipping boy. I believe they would gain also in virtue if they would examine their own tastes more critically: when a good comedian and a production of Hamlet are on rival channels, I wish I could be confident that less than half the professors were laughing.

The main indictment of the intellectual, however, is that the market place operates on the principle of self-interest, and in fact through competition compels even the philanthropic businessman to become self-serving. Self-interest, often described with such neutral words as egotism, greed, and dog-eat-dog, is viewed as a crass, antisocial element of man's character and an economic system that rests upon, and inculcates, this motive achieves little admiration. In fact, a dislike for profit-seeking is one of the few specific attitudes shared by the major religions.

I also find naked selfishness an unendearing trait, but I have trouble in separating it from the more admirable motives related to it. A prudent regard for one's own survival is generally applauded even if the individual does not say, "I got out of the way of the oncoming train only to spare my Sunday School class pain." The violent endeavors of an athlete to defeat his rivals are much admired, providing the contest is more or less fair, even though the winner is expected not to say, "I am glad I won chiefly because I'm vain, but secondarily for the honor of Sheboygan High School."

Even in fields somewhat removed from the athletic arena, the roles of self-interest and what for lack of a better name I shall call benevolence are perplexingly interwoven. I have spent my life among college teachers, although admittedly in the most competitive branch of research and publication. In one sense the disinterest of my colleagues is beyond doubt: I have seen silly people—public officials as well as private, by the way—try to buy opinions but I have not seen or even suspected any cases in which any important economist sold his professional convictions. It is also true that many of the best professors, and many of the worst, could earn more in other callings.

But on the other hand, the motives that drive them and me are not completely clear, either. When we strive to solve a scientific problem, is ambition for our own professional status completely overshadowed by our love of knowledge? I wonder. When we write an article to demonstrate the fallacies of someone else's work, is our hatred for error never mixed with a tiny bit of glee at the display of our own cleverness? I wonder.

To shift elsewhere, I have never encountered a political candidate who said, "I am running for office because I, with my dear wife and future administrative assistant, can earn more in politics than elsewhere." Nor do I expect to. But the language of public interest surely covers a good many acres of self-interest.

A major source of the view that the market place places special values on self-interest, beyond those more or less evident in all human behavior, is the belief that one man's gain is another's loss, that business, like the so-called friendly poker session, is a zero-sum game. Not so.

On the one hand, it must be recognized that the great source of market gains is the productivity of the participants. Unlike the poker game, the wealth of our society has been doubling even on a per capita basis every 25 years, and the doubling has been due to the labors and ingenuity of the men in the market place. Of course there are also incomes achieved by monopoly rather than by efficiency, by fraud rather than by output, but it would be a wholly extravagant estimate that they amount to 10 per cent of the income of the market place. There is room for improvement here, but there is vastly more room to admire the prodigious production achievements of the market place.

On the other hand, I would emphasize that most of the gains from innovation in the market place are passed on to the community at large. A new idea may yield handsome profits for a time, but the rapid rush of competition soon drives the price of the product down to a modest level. Ball-point pens were first marketed at $12.50 to those penmen eager to write under water (and, judging by my experience, only under water); they rapidly fell in price and as you know are now so cheap that you have no economic excuse if you do not write the Great American Novel. Sears, Roebuck and Company and Montgomery Ward made a good deal of money in the process of improving our rural marketing structure, but I am convinced that they did more for the poor farmers of America than the sum total of the federal agricultural support programs of the last 28 years.

It is an interesting illustration of the great influence of the intellectual that the market place itself has become apologetic of its pursuit of profit. The captains of industry now list, in a world in which public relations are becoming as important as efficiency, among their major achievements the great number of bowling alleys or college fellowships they have given to their employees. To boast that large profits demonstrate great efficiency in producing existing products and introducing new ones is considered even by them to be too archaic a form of thought for public consumption. The patron saint of economics, Adam Smith, once wrote

I have never known much good done by those who affected to trade for the public good. It is an affectation, indeed, not very common among merchants, and very few words need be employed in dissuading them from it.

I wonder what those very few words were.

To return to the intellectuals, their dislike for the profit motive of the market place no doubt rests in part on a failure to understand its logic and workings. It is a fact painful to record that the level of economic literacy has not risen noticeably in the twentieth century. Indeed as professional economics becomes more complicated and its practitioners use an increasingly more formidable apparatus, there seems to have been retrogression in our ability to communicate with other intellectuals. Less than a century ago a treatise on economics began with a sentence such as, "Economics is a study of mankind in the ordinary business of life." Today it will often begin, "This unavoidably lengthy treatise is devoted to an examination of an economy in which the second derivatives of the utility function possess a finite number of discontinuities. To keep the problem manageable, I assume that each individual consumes only two goods, and dies after one Robertsonian week. Only elementary mathematical tools such as topology will be employed, incessantly."

But misunderstanding is not the whole explanation: I

cannot believe that any amount of economic training would wholly eliminate the instinctive dislike for a system of organizing economic life through the search for profits. It will still appear to many intellectuals that a system in which men were driven by a reasonably selfless devotion to the welfare of other men would be superior to one in which they sought their own preferment. This ethic is deeply imbedded in the major religions.

I personally also believe that the good society will be populated by people who place a great value on other people's welfare. This is, however, not the only attribute of the good society, and in particular in the good society a man should be free within the widest possible limits of other men's limitations on his beliefs and actions. This great ethic of individual freedom clashes with that of benevolence, for I can seldom do positive good to another person without limiting him. I can, it is true, simply give him money, but even in this extreme case where I seem to place no bonds on him, he inevitably faces the question of what conduct on his part will lead me to give money to him again. Usually I will find it hard to be content to do so little good—giving money to improve a man's food or housing or health will seem as inefficient as giving him gasoline so he will drive more often to museums. Hence when I give money I shall also insist that it be spent on housing, or on medical care for his children, or on growing wheat in the way that I think is socially desirable, or on the collected works of Burke and de Tocqueville, or of Marx and Lenin. A patron tends to be paternalistic, in a nice way, of course. I am not saying that benevolence is bad, but that like everything else it can be carried to excess.

One final question on motives—why are they so important? Am I to admire a man who injures me in an awkward and mistaken attempt to protect me, and to despise a man who to earn a good income performs for me some great and lasting service? Oddly enough, I suspect an answer is that motive makes a difference—that it is less objectionable to be injured by an incompetent benefactor than by a competent villain. But I leave with you the question: are motives as important as effects?

Several charges related to the dominance of self-interest have rounded out the intellectual's indictment of the market place:

First, the system makes no provision for men whose talents and interests are not oriented to profit-seeking economic activity.

Second, there are cumulative tendencies toward increasing inequality of wealth, which—if unchecked—will polarize the society into a great number of poor and a few very rich.

Third, the game in the market place is unfair in that inheritance of property plays an immensely larger role in success than the efforts of the individuals themselves.

I shall comment briefly on each of these assertions.

The first charge is true, the market place will not supply income to a man who will not supply something which people want. People have enormously varied desires, but not enough of them wish to hire men to engage in research on ancient languages nor, sixty years ago, did they hire men to study quantum mechanics. The market place does not provide an air force or alms for the poor. It does not even supply babies. I conclude that a society needs more than a market place.

The second charge, that there are cumulative tendencies to ever-increasing inequality of wealth, is untrue. I would indeed ignore the charge for fear of reprimand from the Society for the Prevention of Cruelty to Straw Men, were it not that this straw man is so popular. In plain historical fact, the inequality in the distribution of income has been diminishing, and the diminution has been due to market forces even more than to governmental efforts. It is also worth noting that a modern market economy has a less unequal income distribution than in either centrally directed or unindustrialized economies.

The third charge, that inheritance of property plays a dominant role in the distribution of income in the market place, is an overstatement. Inheritance of property is important, but it will give some perspective to the charge to notice that property income is only one-fifth of national income, and inherited property is less than half of all property, so less than 10 per cent of all income is governed by inheritance of property.

No useful purpose would be served by trying to appraise the proper role of inheritance of property in a few passing remarks. We should have to look carefully at the effects of inheritance on incentives; we should have to look at gifts during life, which are almost equivalent to bequests; and we should have to decide whether privately endowed colleges do enough good to offset the inevitable high-living heirs— whether we can have Carleton without having Tommy Manville.

But our greatest problem would be that inheritance extends far beyond a safe deposit box full of bonds and stocks. I have told you that you are intelligent; I now add that the chief reason you are intelligent is that your parents are intelligent. Some of you, especially the younger of you, may find this unbelievable: Mark Twain said he was astonished by how much his father had learned during the short time it took Mark to grow from 18 to 21. But inheritance of ability is important, probably more important in its effects on the distribution of income than is the inheritance of property.

So a full account of the proper role of inheritance would have to extend to ability, and perhaps even to name and reputation, as the junior senator from Massachusetts might agree. The social and legal institutions governing inheritance in our society are surely open to improvement, but we are unlikely to improve them if we are guided by nothing more than naive egalitarianism.

And now to my final point. We are great believers in the human mind, we intellectuals, and of its ability to conquer an ever larger part of the immense domain of ignorance. But we have not made much use of the mind in reaching our views on the economic organization appropriate to the good society so far as its basic cultural values go. It is clear that the kinds of traits that are fostered in man are influenced by (but of course not only by) the way economic life is organized—after all, throughout history men have spent half their waking hours in economic activity.

Important as the moral influences of the market place are, they have not been subjected to any real study. The immense proliferation of general education, of scientific progress, and of democracy are all coincidental in time and place with the emergence of the free enterprise system of organizing the market place. I believe this coincidence was not accidental: the economic progress of the past three centuries was both cause and effect of this general growth of freedom. The dominant era of the free market place was in the Nineteenth Century. I believe, but with less confidence, that the absence of major wars in this century—the only peaceable century in history—was related to this reign of liberty. I believe, again with less confidence, that the contemporary transformation of the British public from a violent and unruly people into a population of almost painful Victorian rectitude was related to this reign of liberty.

These beliefs may be right or wrong, but they are not matters of taste. They are hypotheses concerning the relationship between economic and social organization, and are subject to analytical development and empirical testing. It is time that we did so, high time. Our ruling attitude toward the market place has not changed since the time of Plato. Is it not possible that it is time to rethink the question?